THE HISTORY OF SKETCH COMEDY

THE HISTORY OF SKETCH COMEDY

A JOURNEY THROUGH THE ART AND CRAFT OF HUMOR

KEEGAN-MICHAEL KEY
&
ELLE KEY

CHRONICLE BOOKS
SAN FRANCISCO

This book is dedicated to Andrew Eisenman and anyone in a leadership role who allows artists to express their creativity and vision with boundless love and support.

Library of Congress Cataloging-in-Publication Data is available.

ISBN 978-1-7972-1683-6

Manufactured in China.

Jacket and interior art direction by Elle Key.
Jacket design by Elle Key and Gravillis.
Jacket photography by Sally Montana.
Jacket photography hair and makeup by Louie Zakarian and Brittany Hartman.
Illustrations by Elle Key.
Photography credits: Pages 6, 134, 170 courtesy of Getty Images; pages 10, 32, 60, 84, 208, 238, 266 courtesy of Shutterstock; pages 22, 52, 131, 213, 218, 220, 222 courtesy of Keegan-Michael Key and Elle Key; pages 29, 35, 153, 203 courtesy of Comedy Central; page 108 courtesy of Alamy; page 226 courtesy of Kevin Mazur; page 235 courtesy of Jon Pack; page 237 licensed by Warner Bros. Entertainment Inc.

10 9 8 7 6 5 4 3 2

Chronicle books and gifts are available at special quantity discounts to corporations, professional associations, literacy programs, and other organizations. For details and discount information, please contact our premiums department at corporatesales@chroniclebooks.com or at 1-800-759-0190.

Chronicle Books LLC
680 Second Street
San Francisco, California 94107
www.chroniclebooks.com

Contents

Introduction

From the beginning of time, there have been many important questions that have perplexed the human race, such as: *Why are we here? What is the meaning of life?* and *Who's on first?*

Two of these questions, well, they're above my pay grade. But, the last one: now *that* one I actually know a thing or two about.

Comedy is not just part of my profession, it's part of my soul. And I have been lucky enough to spend many years not only performing, but also researching, and teaching, the history of this multifaceted art form.

To start, *Who's on first* is a line from a comedy routine, which has a lot of similarities to a sketch, but it's actually something called *cross talk*, and Abbott and Costello were masters of this kind of performance. And by the way, *Who's on first* isn't a question. It's a statement. Abbott is making up names for the players of an imaginary baseball team. He tells Costello,

Who is on first, What's on second, I dunno's on third.

Costello is confused and responds,

Yeah, that's what I wanna find out.

To which Abbott replies,

Huh, I'm telling you—Who is on first, What's on second, I dunno's on third.

Costello gets more and more heated . . .

You're the manager of this team and you don't know the guys' names?!

Setting up that the *name* of the baseball player on first base is *Who* is something no one was expecting. It's inevitable that they both get more and more frustrated with each other, and the laughs in this routine go on and on for about six more minutes . . . and eighty years . . . and counting.

There are many different types of sketches and different ways they're executed, and together we will take a look at the world of sketch comedy, and ideally answer some easier questions, such as *who* are the people who helped build it, *what* are some of the delicious ingredients they used, *when* did it all start, *where* are we now, and *how* might the future unfold.

What you will find in the pages ahead is a true collaboration of two people who share a passion for comedy and an aligned vision, and who bring complementary strengths to the table. Elle was born in the Bronx and grew up in and around New York City. As a kid, she went with her family to the Catskills (aka the Borscht Belt) and was lucky enough to have the experience of watching performances from comedic greats such as Henny Youngman, Alan King, Robert Klein, and Jackie Mason. She's carried those influences with her and to this day is not one to ever forget a joke. And my girl can conjure up a comedic turn, or turn of phrase, with the best of them. Getting a professional in the comedy world like me to laugh is rare, but that all changed when my path crossed with hers.

As for me, I had a slightly different upbringing and was a child of Detroit. I grew up a block south of 8 Mile Road. Yes, *that* 8 Mile, and miles away from any notion of Hollywood or comedy or sketch. But I always found and appreciated the humor in the life around me. Little did I know at the time that the characters I encountered in my youth would inspire much of the work I would do over the years. There were coaches with anger issues, those pesky and pious sisters who were always putting me in detention. Oh, and there was Pat the wino, who had this deep raspy voice, and Steve the homeless guy I once gave a ride to who bought crack and asked me to wait for him (which I did—I mean, how could I not? Like, I was already there and it would have been too far for him to walk back). And then there were the prostitutes that cheered us on during pickup baseball games at the field at the end of our block.

> *How ya doin', baby? You good? Now you go on, baby, you catch that ball.*
> *SAFE! He safe, baby. Ohhh, he was safe. Ain't that right, Evangeline?*

I collected voices, accents, mannerisms, and even the occasional trick knee. I didn't know it at the time, but I was saving them all for later. For sketches. And as Elle likes to remind me, thankfully I learned my lesson and I never again picked up a homeless crack-head hitchhiker.

In the pages ahead you will not only find the history of sketch comedy and many of its origins and influences, but you'll also get a peek into some of my personal journey as well as a deep dive into some of our favorite sketches. We'll also be sharing with you some anecdotes and pearls of wisdom from friends and colleagues.

And perhaps as we take this journey together, you will laugh with us . . . or even at us . . . along the way.

Either is fine, as long as you're laughing.

CHAPTER 1

The Earth Cooled and Then the Dinosaurs Came

Sketch, as we know and love it today, may only have existed in the last hundred years or so, but the roots of the art form began a long time ago . . . and comedy, well, even longer.

In the Zucker, Abrahams, and Zucker movie *Airplane!*, there is a catastrophic event and Lloyd Bridges' character is very concerned about an airplane that's losing control. He stops a man at the tower (played by the brilliant Stephen Stucker) and demands,

I want to know <u>absolutely everything</u> that's happened up until now.

To which the man thoughtfully responds,

Well, let's see . . . first, the earth cooled and then the dinosaurs came.

And to this day when I'm tasked with starting something at the beginning, I usually think of this indelible Zucker, Abrahams, and Zucker moment and thoughts of dinosaurs. However, starting *The History of Sketch Comedy* with the study of dinosaurs might be a little challenging, as they weren't very funny. Well, maybe the big guy with the little arms, he's kind of funny. I mean come on, his arms are so short. It's like what are you supposed to do with them arms? My man got a big old mouth with all these teeth and the arms don't work. How does he get food up to his face? I can't be the only person who finds the humor in that. Why does he even have the arms? You know what I mean? You know those toy birds . . . the ones that dip in the water? They go sha-bloop and they'd bend over. That's what I imagine a T-Rex had to do to eat.

But my point is short arms or not, he couldn't type or use a pencil so he wasn't able to share with us his comedic shortcomings. Eventually cavemen and women did come along, and I can imagine that *they* had some pretty wacky adventures. Y'all know somewhere there was a dude named Ook, or Magook, who found humor in watching his buddy Gorak try and fail to make a fire or get crushed by a woolly mammoth. And as part of his comedic retelling to the Clan of the Antelope, Magook would break out his best Gorak impression (which I'm sure was spot-on, as Gorak was an easy target considering where he sat on the evolutionary scale).

A sketch, in its most basic form, is a short scene that has characters, a premise, and some sort of comedic escalation or heightening. And, even without the support of those elusive sketch comedy cave paintings—which I'd like to believe are out there somewhere—we can be confident there have been characters and premises since the beginning of the beginning. And escalation, that's not hard to find either.

> *A sketch, in its most basic form, is a short scene that has characters, a premise, and some sort of comedic escalation or heightening.*

Thankfully, one can find actual proof of comedy somewhere around 1900 BCE, in the Middle East, in Sumer. It is in Sumer where the remains of a very special document were uncovered . . . the first evidence of a written joke. Its translation is along the lines of . . .

Something which has never occurred since time immemorial; a young woman did not fart in her husband's lap.

Now, Sumerians were a super impressive group of folks who contributed some pretty amazing things to civilization, so if you were assuming that this first joke was going to be a cunning, and clever, forward-thinking, um . . .

fart joke

then you would be correct.

As for me, that isn't quite what I was expecting from Sumerians. After all, this is the civilization that brought us writing, and the plow, and oh yeah . . . the wheel. No big deal. Writing, the plow, the wheel, and fart jokes. I guess three out of four is pretty good.

Another place in history where there's also a written record of comedy is ancient Greece. It is here we find something historians call "old comedy," which seems appropriate. We're talking somewhere in the world of sixth century BCE, where folks not only *orated* their words but they also thankfully *wrote* their shit down.

The Greeks are credited by many as the creators of theater. Theater and pi: the Greek tragic kind, and the math kind. Thankfully, for those like me who are mathematically challenged but love humor, we can find many of comedy's fruitful seeds in ancient Greece. After all, there were

Jordan Peele

SMELLS OF COMEDY

Bodily functions in comedy tap into something that we repress within ourselves. We pretend we *don't* have penises, vaginas, and buttholes. When someone points it out it makes us cackle. I suppose that the bodily stuff, the taboo of the scatological and all of that "shit" is because the truths we're most ready to pounce on are the things that are repressed within us. And we're taught from this early age (I don't know evolutionarily or whatever) that our bottoms are bad, and poo is stinky, and we're taught to pretend that we don't have those things . . . that we don't have penises and vaginas, that we don't have sex. It's not something that you're supposed to represent in public.

When you tap into something that you're not supposed to talk about, there's an exultation that comes with it. There's an explosion of pent-up energy and pent-up expression that has just been bounding around inside of you. And that is the essence of why comedy and art . . . and fart, is important. Funny and art and fart are the three smells of comedy.

many great playwrights, and plays, and troughs of rich material to pull from. They had backstabbing politicians, brothels, vomitoriums, people throwing dishes, and those husky Spartans thinking everyone else is a wimp. Y'all know those Spartans would just be walking down the street yelling out at the top of their lungs,

THIS IS SPARTA!

I believe that shit's real. Just walking through the 'hood greeting each other.

What's up Homer? THIS IS SPARTA!

In Sparta, I imagine many folks were hard of hearing by the age of twenty-two.

The Greeks also had gods, like multitudes of them. There's Poseidon, god of the sea. Ares, god of war. Hera, goddess of marriage. Athena, goddess of wisdom. And of course, Zeus, the god of the sky, and basically the local rolling stone.

They pretty much had gods for everything you can think of; gods of medicine, of fruits and vegetables, of athletes, of song. There's even a god of sleep: Hypnos. Hysterical. And there were plenty of jokes to be made . . . just maybe don't make fun of Nemesis, because she's the goddess who enacts retribution. (And if you're listening, I'm not writing anything bad about you, Nemesis. No way. I mean, I have a lot of respect for you, and I think that the work that you do is very crucial.)

Maybe don't make fun of Nemesis, because she's the goddess who enacts retribution.

My favorite of the Greek gods (besides you, Nemesis) is Dionysus, and this is with good reason, as he's the god of theater. He also happens to be the god of wine, so if you were a thirsty actor in ancient Greece, you kind of had a one-stop shop on who you were praying to.

It seems he had many fans. In fact, every year, for five days, the city of Athens would throw a huge festival for my boy Dionysus. It was such a massive and meaningful event that during the time of the festival they would even change the name of the city to Dionysia. They would have parades and singing, dancing and reveling. And they also would have theatrical competitions. The playwrights would all get together and have a contest to see who was the better poet-writer. It was straight up like:

> In this corner we have Archimedes, who hails all the way from that grove on the west side of town where they press the olives . . . weighing in with an "I angered the gods, now I'm going to have to sacrifice an offspring." And his opponent tonight is none other than the great Testa-clees . . . weighing in with "one tragedy about sleeping with your momma and two tragedies about killing your dad."

The playwrights would each write three tragedies that actors performed, and they were judged on who was the best. That's right, I said *three* tragedies. And everyone would sit and watch all the tragedies *in a row*. Yes, three whole tragedies, I mean, that's a lot of catharsis.

Then, after the third tragedy, to lighten the mood, they would perform something called a *satyr* play. The satyr plays were usually about Dionysus and his life and his children. They were lighthearted, usually fast paced, and pretty provocative.

The satyr plays were much shorter than the tragedies, and they were funny. I mean, they had dudes in them who were drunken half-men half-goats, and they wore huge phalluses all over the place. Lots of penis humor. They loved penises. I mean of all the genitalia I would agree the penis is the funniest.

The Dionysia festival thing went over so well that eventually they decided to add another festival earlier in the year. This new festival they called the Lenaia. People were digging the satyr plays and comedy so much that they decided that during this festival they would have a comedy competition. The setup was a little different at the comedy contests. They would perform five comedies per playwright. And if you're counting, that works for me. I would happily choose five comedies over three tragedies any day.

Enter the great Aristophanes, who wrote plays seminal to the birth of comedy and had no less than six comedy victories under his belt. He wrote classics that are still performed to this day; plays like *Lysistrata*, *The Birds*, *The Knights*, *The Wasps*, *The Acharnians*, and *The Clouds*. He had the market cornered on the "The"s.

He wrote a comedic play about Dionysus called *The Frogs*. Now, this play is ostensibly about Dionysus complaining that since Aeschylus and Euripides have died, there are no good poets left on Earth. So, he goes to see his half-brother Hercules (yes, half-brother. My man Zeus got around). And he asks Hercules's advice on how to go to Hell and see if he could bring Aeschylus and Euripides back to Earth, since everybody who's left, well, pretty much sucks.

I would happily choose five comedies over three tragedies any day.

I'm not kidding. This is the actual premise for the play. And I know this because I studied Aristophanes in college and was even in the play. I was given the role of Xanthias, who was Dionysus's slave. (And yes, I was the only Black man in the play. And yes, I was cast in the role of *the slave*. And yes, I would love to unpack this . . . perhaps in another book.)

Where was I? Aristophanes. Great playwright. Lots of fun. Up until college I thought all Greek theater was stodgy and tragic, and then I learned that Aristophanes was anything but. I'll give you an example. This is an excerpt from the scene where Dionysus and Xanthias are outside of someone's house and are discussing how to knock on the door.

Now, the Greeks had a tradition of making fun of their gods, even the gods that they prayed to frequently. And in this scene, Dionysus is dressed like Hercules and wearing Hercules's lion tunic. He is also wielding a giant club and he's standing on platform shoes. And he's stalling because he's a fraidy-cat, which is one of the characteristics of Dionysus—he's very much a coward.

DIONYSUS

Let's see—what style do I use at this point? To knock upon the door? Which one to use? What's the local style of knocking here?

XANTHIAS

```
Stop wasting time. Try chewing on the door—
Act like Hercules. You've got his height and might.
```

DIONYSUS
[Knocking]

```
You in there! Doorkeeper!
```

AEACUS
[From inside]

```
Who's there?
```

DIONYSUS

```
I, Hercules the strong!
```

Aeacus bursts through the door and grabs Dionysus very roughly.

AEACUS

```
O you abominable, you shameless reckless wretch—
villain, villain, damned smiling villain—the man who
made off with Cerberus my dog! You grabbed him by the
throat and throttled him, then took off on the run,
while I stood guard. But now I've got thee fast. So
close the Styx's inky-hearted rock, Acheron will hold
you down. Roaming hounds of Cocytus will gnaw your
guts to bits—Echnida, too, and she's a hundred heads.
The Tartesian eel will chew your lungs, your kidneys
bleed from entrails Tithrasian Gorgons rip apart. I'll
set out hot foot in their direction!
```

Aeacus lets go of Dionysus, who drops to the ground in terror. Exit Aeacus back into the house. Dionysus lifts his tunic and inspects his underpants.

XANTHIAS

```
What have you done?
```

I've made an offering. Call the god.

You're being ridiculous. Get up. Move it, before some
stranger spots you.

DIONYSUS

I'm going to faint. Bring the sponge here—set it on my
heart.

Xanthias rummages through the bags and finds a large sponge.

XANTHIAS

Oh, wow, the great "Hercules."
I've found the sponge. Here—you can do it.

Dionysus takes the sponge and begins to clean up his crotch with it.

XANTHIAS

Where are you putting that sponge? O golden gods, you
keep your heart in there?

DIONYSUS

It was scared—it ran off to my lower bowel.

XANTHIAS

Of all gods and men no one's more cowardly than you.

DIONYSUS

Me? How can I be when I asked you for the sponge?
Another man would not have asked, as I did.

XANTHIAS

What would he have done?

DIONYSUS

```
Well, a coward would have lain there and stunk up the
place. But I stood up—and what's more, I wiped myself.
```

XANTHIAS

```
By Poseidon, a valiant act.
```

So . . . it seems that we can thank the Greeks, as the origins of *poop humor* have surfaced. Incredible, right? The earliest known comedy was about flatulence and then poop. Yes, flatulence and poop. And it may seem odd, but I guess it's not that surprising that bodily functions would inspire humor. In school we were always told to "write what you know," and it's a universal truth that everybody poops. So, there you go.

Poop humor has been a go-to for tens, hundreds, make that *thousands* of years. From ancient Greece to the movie *Bridesmaids*, this phenomenon doesn't seem to have . . . *an end* in sight. Yes, I wrote that and I'm proud. I wrote it. I don't give a fuck. I think puns are hilarious.

What is really amazing is that these observations Aristophanes made about human behavior (the things he noticed about politics, and society, and the battle of the sexes) are the seeds of inspiration for many movies, TV shows, and sketches created today. The story lines and plot twists that make us laugh and linger with us—much of that juicy stuff comes from the Greeks.

Okay, I have a question. Have you ever noticed that in movies Greeks and Romans are often played by British actors, like with *English* accents? Why they do that? It's Rome, people. Like, in Italy. I mean, why don't they get Italians to play them? Or at least get the accent right. Come on, I know I'm not alone on this one. Two words: Laurence Olivier. Yes, even him. And even in *Spartacus,* as a Roman, this mutha's *full-on British.* You don't have to believe me. You can check it out for yourself. It's fascinating.

So around the same time, there were also troupes of actors that banded together who we refer to as the Dorian mimes. Now these aren't the kind of mimes that, like, get stuck in a box, or be like looking around the corner or are walking against the wind—which I've never understood. I mean really, like when is the wind that strong? Why would *that* be the stock choice? It really boils my noodle. And don't get me wrong; I like mimes. I studied mime in school and I did a lot of it when I was improvising at The Second City. We

Now these aren't the kind of mimes that, like, get stuck in a box.

called it *object work* instead of mime. I think some people thought it sounded cooler. I think mime is cool. But, at any rate, I just don't understand the walking against the wind. Seriously, like where you live are there sandstorms? I mean really, can't you go do something practical . . . like climb a rope?

Anyhow, these *Dorian* mimes were traveling troupes who would perform short, humorous, comedic scenes, and they are an important part of our sketch comedy history. They were called mimes because they were "mimicking" gods and their stories. The scenes they performed were originally written by a dude named Herodas and were mostly about regular folks doing regular things. Did we mention sex is a regular thing?

To give you an example of his work, there's a scene about a guy named Metro who is having a casual conversation with a gal named Koritto and he asks her where she acquired . . . a dildo. Like you do. And they go on to discuss another dude named Kerdon, who made the dildo in question and who is, it turns out, an accomplished dildomaker. And it seems that he disguises his trade by pretending his shop is a shoe shop. Ahh, how little things change. Hey, I'm on social media, I see those web ads for "hand massagers." (Okay, apologies to the small group of you who are actually purchasing vibrating hand massagers for your hands, but the rest of you know who you are . . .)

Point being, these Dorian mimes were way ahead of their time. I mean by thousands of years. They would even have *women* play the women's roles, which only just finally became the standard in the last century or two . . . (with a few creative exceptions that somehow snuck in like *Mrs. Doubtfire*, *Tootsie*, and *Big Momma*). They also focused on subjects and themes similar to Aristophanes. As they say . . . *if it ain't broke, don't fix it.* And also, as they say . . . *if it's got poop and sex in it, it's going to appeal to the masses.* Okay, that second phrase there might not be as well known as the first one, as I just made it up . . . but, when it comes to sketch comedy, it certainly applies.

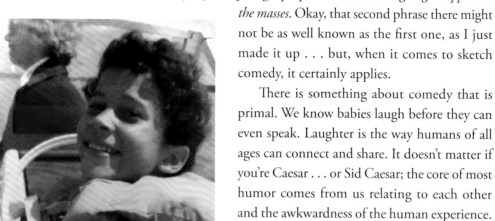

There is something about comedy that is primal. We know babies laugh before they can even speak. Laughter is the way humans of all ages can connect and share. It doesn't matter if you're Caesar . . . or Sid Caesar; the core of most humor comes from us relating to each other and the awkwardness of the human experience.

Greektown

I would like to take you on a journey from the early origins of comedy, way back in Rome and Greece, to a place that is *not so way back*—the home of *my* early origins . . . a block south of 8 Mile in Detroit. Yes, Motown, the Motor City, the D, which is where I grew up. But believe it or not, Greece wasn't totally out of the picture. After all, I lived a short chariot ride away from a place called Greektown. And Coney Dogs, which were served in restaurants owned by Greeks, were a staple of my childhood. There was even a restaurant called The Parthenon. Which, by the way, had excellent moussaka.

I lived in a small house on the border between mostly Black Detroit and the mostly white suburbs. The area has had some notoriety, thanks to the film *8 Mile* starring Eminem. And no, I don't know Eminem, or Berry Gordy, or Stevie Wonder for that matter. I didn't know Marvin Gaye either. I did know Gladys Knight's niece, though. We grew up in the same neighborhood, so maybe that counts for something.

Anyhow, at a very young age, somewhere around when I was three or four years old, my parents told me I was adopted. My understanding of adoption was that the woman who gave birth to me wasn't able to raise me, and my adopted parents picked me to raise as their own. And as a child I always wondered what would happen if these new parents ever decided that they didn't want me either. And now that I'm older and wiser, I'd love to say that I have it all figured out, but that's not exactly true. I know that I'm very lucky to have the home I did, and I appreciate all of the opportunities that have been given to me along the way, but you probably don't need a degree in astrophysics to see that kids who are adopted may at times be faced with a lack of self-worth or can feel like they don't belong or fit in. Maybe even more than others. And I am no exception.

And yes, I do know that astrophysics isn't the right science here, but it's funny to name something that's clearly unexpected. I could have gone with *philately*, which might have been even funnier, as it sounds even more like a social science, but is actually the study of postal stamps. I mean, there are a lot of sciences to pick from. For example, there's pomology, which I only just recently learned is *not* the study of palms. One of my favorites is gigantology, which *is* indeed the study of giants. And frankly, I probably also said astrophysics because it might get a reaction, a smile, a chuckle, or maybe even someone out there might read this and think, Hey, this guy makes mistakes and I make mistakes, so we're similar . . . and I like him for that.

My bigger point is that maybe most, if not all, *-ologists* can figure this one out . . . that when a kid doesn't feel like they belong, they can certainly act out or, well, in my case, act. Whether I was fully aware of it or not, I was constantly trying to figure out what I needed to do to make everybody accept me, and it was certainly reflected in my behavior. Thankfully for me, the energy I put into getting into fights on the

Hey, this guy makes mistakes and I make mistakes, so we're similar . . . and I like him for that.

Ken Jeong

AN ART TO MEDICINE

In college, my major was zoology. It's biology without the botany. And sketch and improv comedy are kind of like running a very artistic diagnostic and trying to figure out something; figure out the truth of the scene. Once you master the science, there is an art to medicine. There are so many times where I have felt in my medical career (this is before I was acting and doing comedy full-time) that medicine is a very skilled and educated improvisation. There is an improv element to medicine that not a lot of people think about. And when you do an improv scene in comedy, you're trying to find the truth of the scene. It's the same thing in medicine. When you're diagnosing a patient, working with a patient long term, you will keep using diagnostics, keep thinking, and keep *educationally improvising* until you get to the truth.

Tracy Morgan

THE GIFT OF HUMOR

When I was going through tough times in my life, comedy saved me and sketch comedy gave me closure. I wrote Woodrow [for *SNL*]. All the girls that I lost, Woodrow helped me get closure from those breakups. These things. You live them. I was in a coma and this season of *The Last O.G.* I was in a coma. It was surreal looking down at myself in a coma. It brought closure to me. I let it go after. Just reliving it. I was able to look at it with appreciation. Our sense of humor, all of us, anyone involved in comedy, that's God. That's the gift he gave us, our sense of humor. God gave all of us involved in comedy senses of humors to deal with the pain. People say a sense of humor comes from pain. No, he gave us senses of humors to deal with it. He gave us senses of humors to deal with the pain. To help us get through all the tough times.

playground, and speaking out of turn in class, did eventually transition into my joining chorus and even landing a role in the school play.

I know I'm not alone on this. A number of my comedic contemporaries today have had a similar path. There are many actors who use this art form as a way to channel their energy into something positive, and something that brings joy to others. Many of my talented peers, from Jim Carrey to Tracy Morgan, have found humor as a path through some darker times. The brilliant and Oscar-winning actor Alan Arkin had such a rough time growing up that he specifically credits his time performing at The Second City for saving his life.

The First Time I Heard My Father Laugh

Even though it was most definitely past my bedtime, it was a rare Saturday that I didn't try my very darndest to sneak back downstairs and catch some of the great *Saturday Night Live*.

The first time I remember hearing my father laugh was in the living room of my childhood home. My father watched the TV screen in awe and in glee. And he was chuckling. My man was chuckling. My father, who was six foot four, 270 pounds, and an otherwise very stoic man, was losing his damn mind. What the hell was happening? It turns out that one of the greatest comedic talents of all time was on TV.

There was magic coming from the screen; it was a scene on *SNL* where Stevie Wonder, yes, that Stevie Wonder ("My Cherie Amour," "Ribbon in the Sky," "Higher Ground," "Superstition") is auditioning for a job as someone who *impersonates* . . . Stevie Wonder. And he starts his impression with a song, and he's doing the whole thing like off-kilter and off-key. It's really funny. He does a truly fantastic job as a terrible singer. He continues to sing and sing badly.

The camera turns to reveal a young and brave sketch comedian named Eddie Murphy.

Then it happened, the camera turns to reveal a young and brave sketch comedian named Eddie Murphy. In the scene, Eddie is playing the executive who is running the audition, and he stops Stevie Wonder and says:

Man, that's the worst Stevie Wonder impression I've ever seen in my life.

And then, Stevie responds in a voice that channels an awkward and high-pitched Jerry Lewis:

What's the matter with it?

Like straight-up Jerry Lewis, he's playing a nerd and he's killing it. Then Eddie, who is clearly frustrated, shares:

Oh man, what you're doing is ridiculous, man. I know Stevie Wonder and what you're doing is . . . it's too tense, man. You need to mellow out a bit.

What came next is one of the most creative, funniest, boldest moves I'd ever seen in my life.

Eddie Murphy reaches into his pocket for something and he says,

Now, the secret to doing Stevie Wonder is . . .

And then this ballsy motherfucker reveals a pair of black sunglasses and goes on to show our Stevie Wonder "impersonator" how to really do a "Stevie Wonder." He's just like,

Man, is Stevie unique. You got to have the glasses and you got to loosen up that neck, man. Move that neck around. Just got to move that neck around a little bit.

And Eddie does his own spot-on version of Stevie, IN FRONT OF THE LEGEND THAT IS STEVIE WONDER. What?!?? And then, get this, Eddie starts singing! Like he's going to sing better than Stevie Wonder. And he does! What the heck . . . ?

My little mind was blown. Ain't nobody in my house was ever the same again. My father and I both drank the giggle juice, and we were done. Finished. Fini. Terminado. Kaput. And if I am ever asked if there was a specific moment that started me on my path toward the mecca of sketch comedy, I would say it was *this* monumental moment, watching this scene, in that little house on Woodstock Drive off of 8 Mile Road. This was the beginning of all of it for me.

Hey You Can't Do That

This brings me to the part of the chapter I'm calling:

Hey you can't do that.

Otherwise known as: *Hey, baby, nuh-uh, you can't do that shit. Y'all crazy.*

It goes a little something like this . . . You know when you're watching a sketch and one of the characters does something really outrageous, something above and beyond, that is just so ridiculous it's probably even wrong? I'm talking about one of those moments that is so out of left field, it should be against the rules . . . like a moment when someone might actually get up out of their seat and talk back to the screen. I've seen brothers during a comedy show that have to go and leave a room because the joke surprised them so much. That's the stuff I'm talking about.

Jordan Peele and I, on our show *Key & Peele*, were keenly aware of this level of response and liked to see it as a challenge; how do we get someone who is watching one of our sketches to get up and say the words out loud,

No. No. This mutha . . . nope, you can't do that . . . y'all stupid.

For our first *Hey You Can't Do That* moment, I would like to share with you a sketch from our show that lives in the time period somewhere between Magook and Hercules.

It's a sketch we call *Severed Head Warriors*. The premise of the sketch is a simple one; there's a war between two groups of barbarians. Like you do. And Jordan and I join forces with a couple of other animal-skin-wearing-early-man savages. During a great battle, Jordan's character bravely and violently defeats the leader of the other barbarian horde. Then with a dramatic raising of his sword, Jordan cuts off the head of his enemy. We are victorious!

Our fearless leader Jordan reaches his hand down and takes a firm grip of his bloody prize. He lifts his enemy's head in the sky and he screams out a war cry of victory. And all of his warriors (including myself) respond with a war cry right back. It's a trope we've all seen many times in movies. Because it works.

We cheer and holler for him and his kill. And this response of ours is clearly exciting to him. So, he decides to try again, and once more he raises the head and again he cries out!

We start thinking, wait, we, um, did this already, but as we are his loyal tribesmen, we're gonna support him and we once again grunt and cheer. Jordan wants more but can see that he's losing his audience. So, in a scramble to keep his men interested, Jordan tries something new. Instead of the simple head-raising (been there, done that), he sticks his hand up into the bottom of the gory, severed head.

Now, the other men and I are certainly curious about what's coming. And with his hand now up in the guy's neck, Jordan pretends to make the head talk. This creepy puppet head gag gets some cheers . . . but Jordan isn't satisfied. So now what's next? His wheels are spinning. It seems that he may have the crowd back, and he certainly doesn't want to lose them again.

His next idea is to take the head and hold it in front of his crotch and pretend to make the head fellate him, much to the chagrin and disapproval of his soldiers. But he can't give up now. So, he tries something else. He holds the head up, but this time he spins the head on his finger like a basketball. For this act, we all cheer wholeheartedly yet again.

Of course, with the cheers being addictive, he boldly continues on with new bits to try . . . when he really should be quitting while he's *ahead*. (Yes, I said it, and goddammit I'm fine with it.)

By the way, I would like to mention that this sketch has no actual dialogue. It's all grunts, growls, cheers, and a lot of nonverbal communication . . . one example being my character's seemingly numerous ways of doing disappointing eye rolls.

As our fearless leader tries out "new material," there are certain things that Jordan does with the head that the men enjoy, and there are other things the men don't like. It's really fun watching his small barbarian brain try to figure out why they're cheering at one bit and not cheering at others.

All of the antics are pretty silly already, but the real *Hey You Can't Do That* moment comes when Jordan realizes he has exhausted most of his bits and he doesn't know what to do next. So, instead of calling it quits, this BARBARIAN from ancient Europe reaches into his blood-soaked tunic and pulls out a little piece of paper. He unfolds it and turns his gaze to the page and mimes through what we realize is a list of the bits he's already done.

While focusing on his ancient stand-up comedy "cheat sheet," he grunts as he goes through shortened versions of his earlier actions so he can figure out what he's missed. The men stand around him and stare with confusion and disappointment as he mimes to himself, *Okay, I did the "spin on the finger," I did the "make the head talk," I did the "make the head give me a blow job," I did the "I now have two heads bit"* . . .

THIS FREAKIN' KILLS ME.

The first time I saw him run through his stand-up comedy CliffsNotes on set, I was off camera. Thank God I was too, because I lost my shit. I got up from my chair, and I had to walk away. Literally. I. Walked. Away. It was absolutely amazing.

I mean who does this?? You can't do this. All of the earlier antics were ridiculous enough—

But ain't no barbarian stand-up comic sneaking a peek at his joke sheet to figure out which severed head bits he ain't done yet.

No. Come on. Na uh. Just no. Jordan kills me. I mean, the dude gets me to crack up a lot, but this one? Nope. This is some *next-level shit* right here. On this one, on this one I had to take me a lap.

You. Can't. Do. That. But he did. Love me some Barbarian Jordan.

CHAPTER 2

I'm Gonna Get Medieval On Ya'

On any given day, there is an office where during a meeting the boss makes a lame joke and a whole bunch of employees laugh uproariously. Whether the boss is actually funny or not is beside the point. Most of the time they're laughing because they fear for their jobs.

And sometimes in those meetings there exists a brave worker who has been taking copious notes, but these notes are not on the PowerPoint. They are collecting material on their superior . . . which will be put to good use later as part of their comedic performance at the proverbial watercooler.

This mocking of the boss by the office funnyman or -woman is a valued tradition, and can manifest in different ways. It can be the performance of physical gestures, like maybe they can do the boss's walk perfectly, or some may be talented enough to do a spot-on vocal impression—all for the glee of their fellow workers.

Imagine, for example, the boss running the meeting says something in the world of,

Um, guys, the second quarter was really good. And as we go into quarter three, I'm going to need you salesmen to leave nothing on the field. Let's give it to them, guys. I mean, for all <u>intensive</u> purposes . . . we're going to make this month one for the bookshelf!

Seriously, my man says some insane misquotes like *one for the bookshelf.* Up here talking 'bout *let's leave nothing on the field . . . ?* You want to leave *nothing* on the field. So, you don't want to make any money next quarter? What is he talking about? C'mon, you *know* that dude exists, and we have all had one boss, or twelve, that in some capacity is an easy target.

What you may not realize is that this lampooning of the hierarchy has been going on for hundreds of years, even as far back as the Middle Ages. Although, if you were part of a king's court in medieval times and you were the one caught doing the mocking, instead of getting severance, you could end up with a severed head.

There was, however, one person who was, for the most part, immune to that unfavorable fate: the court jester. These bold men, and women, were masters of comedy and could get away with mocking the king. As a matter of fact he, or she, was usually hired to do just that. And yes, there were female jesters. At the time, it was actually one of the few professions in which a woman could find work.

One of the most famous female court jesters was a woman named Mathurine. She, along with her infamous razor-sharp wit, performed in the court of three consecutive French kings: Henry III, Henry IV, and Louis XIII. Now Mathurine wasn't only known for her comedy. It seems that one night, someone tried to assassinate Henry IV in his bed and Mathurine blocked the door and kept them from escaping. Due to her quick thinking and quick action, the guy was apprehended and executed.

Good for you, Mathurine, you caught his ass.

She straight up foiled an assassination attempt, and was a hero. Good for you, Mathurine, you caught his ass. She blocked the door and saved the king. That's some impressive shit right there. I'm serious, that kind of bravery I'm not familiar with, because I wouldn't

THE HISTORY OF SKETCH COMEDY

have blocked the door. Heck no. Not me. I would have let him go past. I'd have just been like,

Are you leaving now? See you later. Here's your knife. Enjoy your evening.

Or worse . . .

Good on you for going after the king. Bet you're excited about the upcoming regime change . . . I mean, me too. Yup.

Even without foiling assassination attempts, the jester was one of the first satirists and brave in many ways. I see the jester as an early pioneer of sketch as we know it. Our bold Mathurine, and her other castle clown compatriots, were *allowed* to speak the truth. And these fools or buffoons (as they were sometimes called) would perform for whomever was in the seat of power and were encouraged to make fun of their employer, even to their face.

This type of fodder and gossip was the jester's bread and butter. And even though the king appears to love the ribbing, if the jester goes too far there could be trouble. So, for the jester, figuring out where the line is, well, is pretty important. Shakespeare himself gave us a little insight into the fool's job description. In Act 1 of *King Lear*, the fool in the play shares,

I marvel what kin thou and thy daughters are. They'll have me whipped for speaking true, thou't have me whipped for lying.

So, a bit of a balancing act for the old jester. It's not always super clear where that line is. And, this is something everyone in comedy faces . . . even today. Now I'm not going to get into who is currently in "comedy jail," but I will tell you this, it is a real thing, and many a man (as it's mostly men) are stuck there now. Sadly, there might even be one or two folks in *actual* jail, but let's just say they ain't there for poor joke telling.

The entertainment provided by our ancestor jesters could also come in the form of juggling, and acrobatics, and sometimes a jester might throw into the mix something from what I'd like to call their "special set of skills."

There was a Frenchman in the late 1800s who built an entire career based on farting. My understanding is he was considered a national treasure in France. Ah, the French. His name was Joseph Pujol and he began his career in Marseille where he grew in popularity for his *special* skill. Later, he performed at the famed Moulin Rouge, where he was known as a flatulist or *fartiste*. His stage name was Le Pétomane, and he graciously shared his gift with everyone from Edward, Prince of Wales, and King Leopold of Belgium to Sigmund Freud. It was Freud who once said,

Words are capable of arousing the strongest emotions and prompting all men's actions.

I believe it may also have been Freud who coined the follow-up phrase,

Pull my finger.

THE HISTORY OF SKETCH COMEDY

And I ain't talking about comedic stylings of Liam Neeson (which believe it or not he has). No, I'm referring specifically to a very talented young man who worked in the court of King Henry II, by the name of . . . wait for it,

Roland le Fartere

Okay, you got me. It doesn't matter how fancy the font; my man's name was Roland the Farter. That was the name he went by. And every Christmas, Henry II would have a big bash and my man Roland would do a show for the court, and my understanding is that his big finale consisted of, and I quote,

One jump, one whistle, and one fart.

That's the show. That's the finale. The brilliant and talented Mike Myers once shared with me,

Save the best for last and save the second best for first.

So, I'm guessing that was probably a pretty good jump, right? Maybe even a little click with the heels, a whistle, then . . . fart. Ta-daaah! Brotha, please.

Besides bodily function humor, one of the other methods used to entertain the royals and their constituents was to act out dramatic scenes, in a vein similar to what we call "skits" today. For example, if there was a duchess who was sleeping with a marquis in a castle here, or there, this information could make for some really good *jestorial* inspiration. The jester would then be like,

Oh, did Lady Figgyfarthing enjoy her sausage? Well, I don't know if she partook of hers at the meal today, but I hear that last night she enjoyed the Duke of Worthington's . . .

And then the crowd, they would laugh and cheer and yell out,

Oh, fool, you're so scandalous!

And then everybody's cracking up, except Lady Figgyfarthing, because she doesn't find this funny at all. Can you blame her? Seems now they found out about her and Worthington. But then she sees that the king is laughing, so she has no choice and as he looks over, she giggles as she speaks,

Oh, Your Majesty, your jester is just so . . . amusing.

But she really hates that motherfucking jester. But she can't say anything, right? He's got carte blanche.

This clown, this fool, was a hero of mine. Brave, bold, a risk taker. Many things I aspire to be. And I imagine if I were alive then, and working in the arts, my court routine would go a little something like this,

Welcome, lords and shorties, this is the . . . You Asked for Moor Comedy Show!

That's right! Moor, as in,

I'm BLACK, y'all!

(Okay, so side note: Moors are African Muslims who invaded Spain and Italy, just in case you missed that day in fifth-grade history. Now back to our show.)

You ever wonder why the blacksmith doesn't make more comfortable shoes for horses? You know what I'm talkin' about. Why we only got one style of horse shoes? I mean, y'all got different kinds of shoes . . . and sometimes you got to put them sneakers on. You know what I'm saying? And all the horses got is these hard-ass metal curve things. And they gotta wear that shit on their feet all day? I mean, at least at night maybe they should have some comfort, you know. Like fashion them a slipper or something.

And don't y'all tell me it's a size issue, because, I mean, the king gets to wear slippers to bed, and he as big as a goddamn mastodon. Y'all know that king got big feet. Am I right?

Hey, listen, the king's feet, they is so big, the shoemaker don't even bother cutting or tailoring shit . . . they just strap <u>one whole sheep</u> to the bottom of each foot. Which is more than fine with me, because now I can hear that motherfucker coming from the other side of the castle. My man talking about

. . . BAA . . . BAA . . . BAA.

Hey! You said you wanted Moor, and HERE I AM. Whaaaaaat's uuuuuuuuup! That's a war cry from Africa, y'all. Ain't that right, Lady Figgyfarthing? You know what I'm talking about, gurl. It's too easy. You a easy target. Ain't nobody safe today. Look at the Duke of Worthington looking at me like he gonna kill me. Put your sword down, bitch. You ain't gonna do shit.

Ladies and gentlemen, our great band tonight, Loot to Kill, is here with us. Don't go away, we'll be right back after these messages for mead. Mm-hmm . . . do you want honeyed wine, or well water that gives you dysentery?

The choice is clear . . . delicious mead.

Modern Mead Mongers

Even though there are aspects of sketch involved, my understanding is the jester for the most part flew solo. He (or she) wasn't known for having writing partners, or other actors to work off of. It was more of a one-man show, like Chris Rock at Madison Square Garden.

Today we don't have to look far to find the modern relatives of the jester. It's almost impossible to turn on the TV or go online without watching a talk show host lampoon our current leaders. We also have plenty of modern-day versions of jester-type roastings available for our viewing pleasure. You know how they do those specials on Comedy Central where there's some huge celebrity who is surrounded by a bunch of their friends and comedians who tell cruel jokes about them? Maybe they're not royalty in the traditional sense, but there are certainly actors today that are treated as such, and when the opportunity presents itself, many of our Hollywood kings and queens are surprisingly game for a good roast.

The ground-breaking and rule-breaking actor and comedian Zach Galifianakis is the host of a very clever parody of a talk show, called *Between Two Ferns*, where the guests on the show get mocked and ridiculed. They show up as they would to any other talk show, but here they come in *knowing* they will get skewered by Zach and his scathing and condescending comments. These interviews are cut together as short two-person comedic performances, and they are fantastic. One of my favorite episodes of *Between Two Ferns* features Bruce Willis as the guest. Zach starts the bit by introducing him as "movie star and *harmonicist*" and the hits continue from there . . .

> *When you were making [your film]* The Whole Ten Yards, *were you ever worried it would be* <u>too</u> *good?*

> *Did you know that some actors <u>turn down</u> roles?*

> *Where do you keep your Oscar trophy . . . oh, I mean your . . . Blockbuster Entertainment Award?*

Every episode is brilliant and brutal. Another brave guest on the show was Brad Pitt. Clearly there's a lot for Zach to work with here as well . . .

> *How old were you when you lost your virginity? Zero?*

> *Showers. Why don't you take them?*

> *Is it hard for you to maintain your tan . . . because you live in your wife's shadow?*

Perhaps for big stars, not unlike former kings, it's rare to find people who are brave enough to tell it to you straight. And Zach brings it all and then some.

Carol Burnett

THE AUDIENCE WAS MY PARTNER

The thing is, I never could do stand-up. I'm terrified of getting up and being by myself. I always wanted to lock eyeballs with people.

I do remember very early on, on *The Garry Moore Show*, one of the guests was an old vaudevillian named Ed Wynn (he was in *Mary Poppins* and the *Ziegfeld Follies* way back). So, he was a guest this one week and he was in his late seventies, maybe early eighties, and we're sitting around talking and he says,

> *You know the difference between a comic and comic actor? Well, a comic says funny things (like Bob Hope) and a comedic actor says things funny (like Jack Benny).*

And so, I thought, that's what I wanna be; I wanna *say things funny*. That really hit me at home. That's it. That's what I want to do.

We did all kinds of sketches on Garry's show, which gave me my training.

I never wanted to be "myself." I was always more comfortable being in a wig, blacking out my teeth, wearing a fat suit, you know, and then I was comfortable.

When I was going to do my show, the executive producer Bob Banner said,

> *Carol, you know, instead of hiring a warm-up comedian to come out and warm up the studio audience, you should go out and do it. And do a Q & A . . .*

And I said,

> *Oh my God, no! What!?*

BOB

> *Well because they should get to know you before you start putting on all those different outfits and being different people.*

I was terrified. What if nobody asks a question, OR what if they do and I don't have an answer?

I thought, you know what . . . if I have egg on my face at least they'll know it's honest. So, I agreed, and told him we'll do it for three or four weeks and then if it doesn't work, we'll just eighty-six the whole idea.

I remember that first show, I was terrified. And it shows, I mean, it's really funny. And after this aired for about three or four weeks, people saw it and then they would come in ready to ask questions.

And I don't think that's stand-up, because they were my partners. And after a while it became one of my favorite things to do. But that's the only time I was ever alone, but I wasn't . . . because the audience was my partner.

Another master of the modern-day roast is comedian Jeff Ross. We even call Jeff "The Roastmaster General." He truly is one of the best practitioners of the science of roasting we have today. He's a fantastic example of a modern court jester. If our country had a king right now, this is who they would bring in to helm that roasting. And if he needed any help, Stephen Colbert, Jimmy Kimmel, and Jimmy Fallon are just a few of our modern court jesters as well, and they are all out there creatively speaking comedy truth to power.

A Cast of Characters

Years after our medieval jester ruled the court, and when one fool wasn't enough, a band of fools joined forces in something called *commedia dell'arte*. These groups were influential sketch comedy originators, and became key in the who's who of sketch characters. The actors in the commedia created stories, plots, and characters that became seeds for many of the sketch comedy trees that we are still picking our fruit from today.

The commedia was formed in Italy in the sixteenth century. It wasn't long before there were traveling troupes of actors all over Europe who would perform this new and very special style of theater. One of the most important attributes of the commedia was how they used the same cast of characters in most, if not all, of their plays. This is very different from our modern theatrical playwrights who create diverse and varied characters for each of their stories.

Seeing commedia performances was kind of like watching a sitcom or a Bugs Bunny cartoon today. Each show may have a different plot, but Bugs is always there, is always called Bugs, and he is always surrounded by some version of the same backup players. His "troupe" includes folks such as Daffy Duck, Porky Pig, and Yosemite Sam, all of whom keep coming back episode after episode to team up for new adventures. It doesn't matter whether the story you're watching takes place in a haunted house or the Wild West; you know all the characters, and you know what to expect from them as well. Daffy Duck is always a self-described greedy coward, Porky Pig is always the flustered "everyman," and Bugs is always the smart-witted wise guy . . . and usually is nibbling on the same large orange vegetable prop.

I was in an acting class in college when I first heard about the commedia. Our professor came out onto the stage with a bag and set it down next to him. Out of the bag he pulled several masks, or half masks to be exact.

Perhaps you've seen this kind of thing at a masquerade ball? Or maybe you've seen one in a movie where there's a masquerade ball. The masks I'm referring to only partially cover someone's face, like from their forehead to their nose, leaving their mouth and chin exposed.

I was enthralled. Each mask he displayed was unique. One of them had a big round nose, while another had cat-like eyes, and another one had a very long nose that curled down. The masks kept coming, and each was more interesting than the last. We learned that all the distinct masks represented different characters from the commedia, and when an actor wears one, he or she is tasked to embody the character it represents.

Our professor went one by one through their character names and personality traits. After his explanation, he put on each mask and performed for us his interpretations. He started with Pantalone. He donned the mask and began to walk around the room with his back hunched over and his head jutting forward, which accentuated the mask's already very prominent beak. He then scurried offstage, and shortly returned with his old self restored. He went through a similar process with every magical item he pulled from the bag.

For a sketch writer and performer, studying the commedia can be invaluable. These ancient comedic relatives of ours can be found in many of the movies, plays, and sketches we watch and love today. There are even names for the categories the characters fall into.

For example, there are the *vecchi*, who are the people in power and are usually mean, scheming old men. (Our new friend Pantalone fits in this group.) When you're watching a TV show or a movie and you see a self-involved, despicable character like George Costanza from *Seinfeld* or Mr. Burns from *The Simpsons*, you are looking back through time at the commedia, and the tradition of Pantalone.

There's the Dottore. The Dottore is a blowhard who acts like he's smarter than he is. Everyone has met some version of this guy along the way; he's the dude who knows some really big words, but uses them incorrectly. In this case, we're talking about characters like Ron Burgundy (Will Ferrell's character in *Anchorman*) or Michael Scott (Steve Carell's character in *The Office*). These are both super solid examples of modern characters influenced by Dottore.

Next, we have the *zanni*, who are the servants. They work for the vecchi. One of their most popular characters is named Arlecchino. Now Arlecchino was not only a popular zanni, but he may also have been the most popular character in all of commedia. Arlecchino was always coming up with schemes to avoid work or get out of trouble. He was quick on his feet and super energetic. Usually Arlecchino was played by someone who was very athletic and capable of doing stunts and pratfalls. So, if someone had a background in acrobatics they were often cast as Arlecchino. Today, when you see a fast-talking-street-smart-character, like Axel Foley in *Beverly Hills Cop*, or Steve Urkel from *Family Matters*, or our friend Bugs Bunny, you are watching a modern-day version of Arlecchino.

There were female zanni as well. Perhaps the most popular was Columbina. She was the sassy and quick-witted maid. If you have ever seen Fran Drescher in the TV show *The Nanny*, or Florence from *The Jeffersons*, you're watching the undaunted descendants of Columbina. Even Alice from *The Brady Bunch* was known for some sassy Columbina comebacks.

Another group is called the *capitani*, and contains the "brave" Capitano. He was a Spanish soldier who was always sharing his courageous tales of battle. And this motherfucker would just be talking about,

> *I did this at the battle of that. And I was the hero of the battle of this. And I slayed this whatchamacallit here . . .*

And what's interesting is that he would be talkin' all this bravado shit about all the battles he was in, and then you'd find out later that he didn't actually fight in *any* of these battles at all, and that he's a complete and utter coward. The character that comes to mind for me is the Cowardly Lion from *The Wizard of Oz*. He's a perfect example of a Capitano. He roars and he roars to try to scare Dorothy, but we all learn soon enough that he's actually afraid of his own shadow.

Even Alice from The Brady Bunch *was known for some sassy Columbina comebacks.*

The final group is called the *innamorati*. They are the young lovers who are desperately and painfully infatuated with each other. And many of the types of characters I mentioned previously are usually trying to either keep these two together, or tear them apart. For example, if you're watching a movie and there's a miser (a Pantalone) whose daughter has a suitor, you know that he's going to cause trouble for his future son-in-law. Have you seen *Meet the Fockers* or *Crazy Rich Asians*? Both straight-up stories of innamorati.

You can probably figure out who the most famously referenced example of the innamorati is . . .

Any guesses?

Now, if you're thinking "Jim and Pam from *The Office*" I'm going to say sorry, no, but close. The answer we are looking for is . . .

Romeo and Juliet.

Yes, those wacky kids are innamorati, or at least they were, 'til the bitter end. And it was a bitter end because they were so in love and couldn't live without each other that they went and did this messed-up murder-suicide thing. And if I just spoiled the ending for you, I'm not sorry. The tale of *Romeo and Juliet* has been around for like four hundred years and you really should have read it by now. (And on that note, "Rosebud" was the name of the sled, and why not while I'm at it, Bruce Willis was a ghost.)

Now, here comes the really cool part: when it comes to my personal work in sketch comedy and improvisation, once I studied the commedia, it became easy for me to look at what was unfolding onstage in front of me and jump right in. I could step out under the lights and decide to play Pantalone. Boom. I'll be the miser and I'll hoard all of my things and be stingy. And then I'll play the Dottore over here and I'm just going to talk shit like I know what I'm talking about, but I don't really know what I'm talking about.

And the best thing is, most of the folks I improvise with also know these characters, and they can jump in with me. It's kinda like being in the NFL Pro Bowl. Each year, many of the league's best players show up for a football game and play with folks they have never been on the same team with, but these games are terrific to watch and the players all work together really well. Because, like actors who study the commedia, it doesn't matter what school or city you play for; every team studies from a very similar *book of plays*, and they have characters who fall into specific roles, like a quarterback, a kicker, or a defensive tackle. And they all support each other on their grassy stage in order to win the game.

So, if you and your fellow improvisers have studied up on the commedia, it's pretty easy to make some quick choices about who everyone is and how everyone can relate to each other, mask or no mask. If you can figure out who is in each position and everyone has learned something from that same playbook, then you'll all be winning . . . and scoring comedic touchdowns in no time.

Comedy Bits

The creative plots our beloved *commedians* sewed were the threads on which they strung their pearls. Those pearls would be improvisations, sketches, and short bits or scenes, known as the *lazzi* (which is a sexy Italian word for bits). And you don't-a gotta no comedy without bits.

There were stock lazzi that were used by all the troupes across Europe. And even if you've never heard of lazzi, I would bet that you're still probably familiar with the setups of many of them. After all, they're staples of comedy and sketch, and there are all kinds of lazzi that we draw from today.

To start, here's a simple one: *the interruption of the performance lazzo* (*lazzo*, by the way, is the singular of *lazzi*). In this lazzo, a member of the cast who was already onstage goes out and wanders through the audience, and heckles the other actors while they're performing. He or she then might start complaining aloud . . .

You know what, I'm done. I'm absolutely done. I'm not going to be in the play anymore.

They may even find themselves a seat next to a member of the audience and futz with them, and grab their program, and continue,

What? This actor is in this play? That guy stinks. Oh, boy, there he is. There he is right there. Boo. Oh my God, this plot is so thin. Who in the world wrote this thing? Carlo Goldoni? What a hack.

Another more common one you may be familiar with is something known as a *messenger lazzo* where two characters are having a lovers' quarrel and a third character wants to help them patch it up. So, he or she agrees to send messages between them, and then usually a very challenging game of telephone ensues.

There's something called the *lazzo of the fly*. This is where a servant character promises the master that there *isn't a fly in the house* (meaning, there's nothing in the house). And when the master goes and opens the door, he finds that his home is packed with people. And then the servant looks at him, shrugs his shoulders, and with a smirk says,

See, no flies.

Sure, it could be flies, it could be monkeys in the house . . . wherever that person is, the gist of the joke is that they're going to open the door, and everybody is going to be in the house.

And then we have the oh-so-clever *rising dagger lazzo*. That's the bit where, let's say, a character hears about the physical attributes of a woman— how buxom she is, or how shapely she is—and then slowly the sword by his side begins to rise. Ah yes, for better or worse this kind of "elevated" humor stands the test of time.

Today, we have boundless examples of modern takes on lazzi. There's a fun moment in the movie *Beverly Hills Cop* when Axel Foley (who wants to lose the cops that have been following him) decides to have some fancy hotel room service delivered to their stakeout. And while the cops

Mike Myers

EVIL SOUP OF THE DAY

For me, it's always a choice of *wouldn't it be funny if* or *isn't it funny that*. Here's an example: Isn't it funny that every nationality in Europe has their own obsession of a body function? The French: the liver. The Germans: the circulation, and the English: their bowels. And that's true . . . isn't it funny that . . . ?

Wouldn't it be funny if may sometimes stray from more truthful offerings and get into what they call at The Second City "awful fiction," which is something that would never happen. Wouldn't it be funny if Godzilla and Bigfoot live together? You know what I mean?

Isn't it funny that airline flight attendants say "Buh-bye" as you leave the plane. And there's that David Spade sketch which I love: "Buh-bye." You know what I mean? Buh-bye. *Buh-bye.*

I guess I am probably drawn more to *isn't it funny that* than *wouldn't it be funny if,* but having said that . . . wouldn't it be funny if the evil guy is a single parent and has issues with his son, Scott Evil. We are usually spared any actual logistics of a very, very logistically driven organization. But you know, there has to be a cafeteria. There has to be an "evil soup of the day." Wouldn't it be funny if . . .

are preoccupied by the food order, Axel sneaks around behind them and stuffs a few bananas into their car's tailpipe so when they try to follow him their car shakes and breaks down. I guess one could call this a *banana in a tailpipe lazzo* or more broadly *using food as a way of stalling lazzo.*

In the film *Cop Out*, with Tracy Morgan and Bruce Willis, there is a truly wonderful lazzo that caught me off guard. Bruce and Tracy play cops who arrest a thief played by Seann William Scott, and they have him in the back seat of their car. Seann starts goading them and when Tracy tells him to shut up Seann says "Shut up" pretty much in unison with him. And then when Tracy says shut up again, Seann does it again. Tracy and Seann continue speaking over each other like obnoxious children,

Shut up. Shut up . . . Sh/Shut up . . . Shu-Shut up . . . Shut up.

One thing I love about this lazzo is that at one point in the scene Tracy literally speaks to what the game of the lazzo is. While Seann is doing this silly same-time repeating thing, Tracy actually says,

Stop repeating me. Stop repeating m—

And of course, Seann again jumps on that and tries to match Tracy here too. Thanks to Tracy I guess we can call this one the *stop repeating me lazzo.*

Another modern-ish lazzo that I really love takes place on a television show from the '70s called *Laverne & Shirley*. Michael McKean and David Lander are the actors who played the characters Lenny and Squiggy, and they had these incredible, what I'm calling *entrance lazzi* on the show. The setup pretty much followed the same format. Laverne, who was played by Penny Marshall, and Shirley, who was played by Cindy Williams, would be in their apartment sitting on the sofa sharing some episode exposition, and something would inspire Shirley to have a line of dialogue in the world of,

Well, I think that might be the most disgusting thing I've ever seen.

And then the front door dramatically swings open, and the very awkward and wacky team of Lenny and Squiggy would pop in right on cue and say,

THE HISTORY OF SKETCH COMEDY

Hello!

On another episode Shirley would say,

If we let our spirits down now, it would be nothing but pure stupidity . . .

Then once again on cue the boys burst in—

Hello!

It's a super fun bit, and once you understand the setup of this lazzo, when you hear one of the girls say a line about something being gross or dumb, you can relish the glee of knowing what is about come.

Lenny and Squiggy would pop in right on cue and say, Hello!

Swords and Waffle Fries

During my college years, I went on a study abroad program to Greece, yes, of all places, and met a lovely man named Todd Hissong. He invited me to work with him back home at the Michigan Renaissance Festival. I accepted, and spent many a sweaty afternoon in Todd's backyard learning the basic moves of stage combat and sword fighting to prepare me for a comedy show that we would perform at the faire. I know that I just interchanged faire and festival, and I'm not sure why I do that. I guess maybe it's because to me "faire" seems very 1980s crafty, and "festival" invokes a 2000s Phish concert, but it's all pretty much the same thing.

Thousands of people would turn out at the faire/festival every weekend. And they'd be in straight-up jean short-shorts, and they would buy beer, and turkey legs, and stuff their face with waffle fries, which is very period. Okay, so maybe they didn't

have waffle fries in the 1400s. But they should have. Anything is better than mead . . . which by the way, was sold at the faire. You could also buy handcrafted on-theme trinkets like little wooden swords and shields for the kids and, of course, drink big ol' red Solo cups of ale.

Okay, so check this shit out. This is some ridiculousness right here. One summer, some Rhodes Scholar thought it would be a wonderful idea to sell *real* swords to adults. Did I mention there was a pub where they sold *real* ale? So, we talkin' about booze and weapons. Just so you understand, this sharp sword sales scenario lasted two days. Which is about, let me see, math . . . carry the one . . . yup, that's exactly . . . *two days* longer than they should have. How you gonna be serving beer to a motherfucker for hours and hours on end in the hot sun and then say,

Before you stumble out into the crowd, good sir, would you care for a sharp and deadly sword?

Thankfully they put an end to this before the local news had stories talkin' 'bout . . .

Tonight, a man decapitated at the Michigan Renaissance Festival in Grand Blanc. News at seven.

At any rate, the rest of the experience was awesome. I was surrounded by tightrope walkers, fire eaters, belly dancers. And from every corner of our small imaginary town of Hollygrove, you would find people practicing arts that were hundreds of years old. It was magical.

The show that Todd and I performed had a very traditional feel to it: lots of quips, banter, and physical comedy. I also had the opportunity to do street theater, which allowed me to interact with the patrons at the

THE HISTORY OF SKETCH COMEDY

festival. One bit that always worked particularly well on a damp day was to find someone armed with a camcorder . . . You remember those? You remember those big-ass cameras people used to carry all the time? I would walk up to the lens and say,

Welcome to foggy London.

And then I would breathe heartily into the camera, fogging up the lens. And it was good, clean fun that went over much better than it should have.

Another chestnut was the empty stroller gag. Someone would be taking in the sights, and they're walking through the festival, and they're pushing a stroller with nothing in it (because their spouse would be holding the child). And then Todd, he would run up with a dire sense of urgency and he'd say,

Sir, go back! You left the child in the car!! You've left the child!!

So now, I know what you're thinking . . . if we're playing characters from the Renaissance, how does Todd know what a car is? And I'm not . . . I'm just not really sure how to answer that except by saying that we chose to adapt to our surroundings and improvise with what we had . . . like camcorders and red Solo cups. Ah, the '80s.

I soon discovered that many of the things we did were stock bits, and not unlike our friends at the commedia, or at the NFL, these bits had been handed down from one group of folks to the next at various festivals throughout the years.

It was here where I honed some of my comedic chops, learned some clowning techniques and pratfalls, along with other skills and tools for me to put in my newly purchased Renaissance faire comedy basket. And yes, I bought it at a place called Ye Ol' Baskets.

Step right up and buy one of our handmade baskets. Ye Ol' Baskets.
Our baskets are . . . unbeweavable.

Yes, I'm sorry, that one was painful. But, you know what . . . if y'all were in an office, and I was your boss right now though, you'd be fake-laughing your asses off.

Matt Lucas

COMEDY DUO NUGGETS

When David Walliams and I were writing together on *Little Britain* we'd sort of start on opposite ends of the line and meet in the middle. And what David was really, really, really good at was coming up with a pure comic concept. And I think my strength was in the textures, the cadences, the accents, the rhythms . . . the characterizations. I realized that by working together so much, and so closely, and for so long, we sort of learned each other's techniques. What you gain in partnership is much greater than what you do on your own.

Every sketch you ever saw about the hypnotist Kenny Craig was written by the two of us and was equal. One of my favorite concepts was that Kenny uses his powers offstage, but for very small gain. We both loved the idea that someone can have all this hypnotic power, but their imagination, their ambition, didn't really extend. For example: Kenny would walk into a McDonald's and say,

> *"In a moment I will ask for six Chicken McNuggets.*
>
> *You will place nine Chicken McNuggets in the box . . ."*

Hey You Can't Do That

This brings us to our second *Hey You Can't Do That* moment, which comes from one of the greatest "sketch comedy" movies of all time, *Monty Python and the Holy Grail*. Now, if you haven't seen this film, and you're a fan of sketch, drop everything and run to your nearest . . . okay, I'm sorry, after you finish reading this book, you can run . . . well, maybe don't run. You can walk. Or don't even get up from where you are. You can probably just stream it on whatever is nearby or in front of you.

However you can do it, you must see this film. It has everything. It has a medieval king that's a Pantalone who's trying to marry his son off to win a lot of land. It has a Capitano who loses his head . . . oh, wait, no, he loses everything *but* his head. It has rude Frenchmen, killer rabbits, God is in it. I'm telling you, it's jam-packed. It even has farts. God and farts . . . ? See, everything.

It's so epic, there are entire books out there written about this one movie. It is a film with a plot, and has a connected story line. However, almost every scene in this brilliant masterpiece could be viewed on its own as a sketch as we know it—with characters, a location, obstacles, and a setup that heightens. And there are almost *too many* incredible lazzi. That's a joke. There's no such thing as too many bits, at least not when your screen is blessed with the likes of John Cleese, Eric Idle, Terry Jones, Terry Gilliam, and Michael Palin.

> *It has rude Frenchmen, killer rabbits, God is in it. I'm telling you, it's jam-packed. It even has farts. God and farts . . . ? See, everything.*

I do want to share with you one very popular scene from the film where the local *body-monger* (which is what I believe they would call him) is coming through the town to collect the bodies of anyone who has died from a plague or otherwise. He pushes a large wheelbarrow, and stacks the dead bodies on top of each other, as he slowly meanders through the streets.

Along the way he calls out,

Bring out yer dead!

He's got this bell in his hand and rings it. Then again we hear,

Bring out yer dead . . . bring out yer dead!

Basically, he's like a dead body garbage man. And more and more bodies are brought to his barrow along the way. The fun and games begin when a large man approaches him carrying another smaller man over his shoulder. He addresses the body-monger,

Here's one.

The body-monger asks for nine pence to take the body away. The large man goes to get out his money and there's a high-pitched and confused voice that says,

. . . I'm not dead.

And we realize the words are coming from the dude he's trying to get rid of. But, the guy just spoke. Now, I'm no doctor, but I'mma say . . . he ain't dead.

Now, this is the time when y'all should put that dude down and apologize. I mean, I would. But no, not this fella. The body-monger is as confused as we are.

What?

And the big guy's response is,

Nothing, nothing. Here's your nine pence.

And the dead dude responds,

```
        I'm not dead.

                    BODY-MONGER
        He says he's not dead.
```

                            BIG GUY

          Yes, he is.

                            DEAD DUDE

          I'm not.

                           BODY-MONGER

          He isn't.

Now, I don't know about you, but I would really like to know who is
this motherfucker he's trying to get rid of. And why.

                            BIG GUY

          Well, he will be soon. He's very ill.

                            DEAD DUDE

          But I'm getting better . . .

                            BIG GUY

          No, you're not. You'll be stone dead in a moment.

And the negotiation goes on like this back and forth, and back and
forth. It's sheer insanity. Brilliant. Insanity.

                           BODY-MONGER

          I can't take him.

                            DEAD DUDE

          I feel fine.

The big guy even tries pleading . . .

          Please. Well, do us a favor.

                           BODY-MONGER

          I can't.

                        BIG GUY
```
Well, can you hang around a couple of minutes, he
won't be long.
```

                       BODY-MONGER
```
No, no, I got to go to the Robinsons'. They've lost
nine today.
```

They lost *nine*. So, he's got extra bodies to pick up. Busy day.

                        BIG GUY
```
Well, when's the next round?
```

                       BODY-MONGER
```
Thursday.
```

                       DEAD DUDE
```
I think I'll go for a walk.
```

                        BIG GUY
```
No, you're not fooling anyone.
```

                    [To the Body-Monger]
```
Look, isn't there something you can do?
```

                       DEAD DUDE
            [With as much glee as he can muster]
```
I feel happy! I'm happy!
```

This idiot talkin' 'bout, "I'm happy." Brotha, please.

So, now the body-monger, he doesn't know what to do, so he looks around, takes out a club, and he slugs the skinny guy in the head. And he goes limp and he finally dies.

And then the big guy is like,

Oh, thanks very much.

And the body-monger puts the little dude on the cart like no big deal.

Not at all. See you on Thursday.

What the what?! My man said, "I'm not dead." "Yes, he is." You can't do that. You can't just be throwing people on the dead pile when they ain't dead! The guy just talked, he can't be dead. "I feel happy." No, you can't do that. You know what, that's some crazy-ass writing right there. I'm in awe. It's like the Pythons all fell out of the brilliant tree and hit every clever branch on the way down.

Oh, and then get this, at the very end of the scene, King Arthur comes riding in, and everybody's talkin' 'bout,

Oh, who's that then?

And some dude in a field goes,

I don't know, must be a king.

The other guy with him says,

Why?

And he goes,

Because he doesn't have shit all over him.

That's the answer to the question.

That's how fucked up the Middle Ages were. You either had shit all over you, or you didn't have shit all over you . . . is how you compared people. You *have* shit all over you? Oh, no, you don't? Okay, then you must be a king.

Love me everything about Monty Python.

Monty Python . . . is . . . my . . . shite.

CHAPTER 3

Variety Is the Spice of Life

Variety entertainment is the art form that essentially gave birth to sketch as we know it today. But, before we journey to vaudeville and the luscious and lewd ladies of burlesque, I would like to share a few words about something perhaps even more provocative: corporate theater.

Ah yes, the mandatory company retreat. Spending time with your fellow coworkers, and learning more about them than you ever wanted or needed to know. These mandatory corporate gatherings bring industry colleagues together for team building, skill sharing, and extraordinarily long, dry speeches from company leadership. However, it's not all work, work, work at these things. Sometimes if you're lucky, there may be events with themes like Cowboy Day, or you could win a prize for the best robot costume during the *Who Knows Their Company's Nuts and Bolts* trivia game.

Now I have been lucky enough to participate in a number of these weekends. And because of *my* special set of skills, I am usually at these events to help rally the troops, or share the launch of a new product and press some flesh, as they say. And for the uninitiated, corporate theater can actually be a fascinating thing, at least when it comes to the history of sketch comedy.

Picture this: You're at a conference about ball bearings or new laminate composites to use for kitchen sink tops (something really exciting). And

And for the uninitiated, corporate theater can actually be a fascinating thing, at least when it comes to the history of sketch comedy.

you promise yourself that if you hear one more presentation about carbon and its molecular stability, you're going to look for a new line of work. Not so fast. Enter the corporate show, the entertainment portion of the conference. This could be in the form of a game, like we mentioned, or a funny song about their competition in the industry. Or it could be a sketch that calls out fellow coworkers like *Susan in human resources with her Aerosmith scarves and her Whitesnake poster.* To which a very excited Susan calls out from the audience,

Here I go again on my own! Whooo! Ha, ha, ha. I love Whitesnake! I'm forty-seven.

Thank you, Susan. That was very specific.
Perhaps there's a scene where someone makes fun of Jim in sales.

Hey, I'm Jim! That's me!

. . . and how Jim is eating everybody else's bagels "by accident." Laughter from the audience ensues and other voices call out . . .

Yeah, Jim does do that!

Yep, I do that.

These moments of levity distract from the monotony of the day as well as bring some energy to the room before the upcoming ninety-seven-minute speech everyone will be forced to sit through given by . . . I don't know, let's say, Bob the CEO.

Hey, that's me!

Look, I wouldn't be surprised if by now you're thinking: *Keegan, why are we at a corporate convention in Minneapolis?* Well, I will tell you. Because the methodology behind the format of this kind of event is pretty darn clever, and the brilliant minds that came up with the idea of hyping up the crowd with variety acts should be lauded. And no, I am not referring to anybody on the board. I'm talking about a man by the name of *William Dunlap*!

[Silence from the crowd]

No? So, nobody is going to yell out?

Well, that makes sense because he's not at the conference. 'Cause he died. Somewhere around two hundred–plus years ago.

Okay, so here's the deal, in 1789, William Dunlap wrote a short play called *Darby's Return*. It was meant to act as kind of a filler to run in between the acts of a longer drama. This became a common practice at the time—to have these little interstitial plays where folks would take the stage to keep the audience entertained while the main play would be going through some elaborate set change behind them on the other side of the curtain. Think of it like halftime at a Lakers game. Basically, it's the Age of Enlightenment version of an elaborate cheerleader routine, or of fans being pulled to center court to try to make three-pointers.

Back in the early 1800s, these intermittent acts were so popular that they *became* the show.

Variety entertainment is like only eating the double stuff and throwing away the cookie . . . which is, by the way, how you should do it. I mean, ain't nobody in their right mind eats the cookie and throws away the cream. Because if y'all gonna do that, then you might as well just go buy a *cookie*. It doesn't make any goddamn sense, especially when they put double stuff in there. They put *double the stuff*.

> *Variety entertainment is like only eating the double stuff and throwing away the cookie.*

And you know what, if you're buying Oreos and just eating the cookie, you're probably also the same person who didn't dress up on Cowboy Day.

Cowboy Day is stupid!

I beg to differ.

Mel Brooks

REFERENCES

The word I'm looking for is *references*. In order for a sketch to work, you need references. For instance, the first sketch I ever wrote was for *New Faces 1952*. It was a takeoff of *Death of a Salesman*, and that was a pretty narrow reference. But, it was for a Broadway show, so it was a Broadway reference. It was the second year of a very big hit. *Death of a Salesman* was very big . . . Mildred Dunnock, Lee J. Cobb, and it was just *really* big, and I wrote a takeoff of it. Alice Ghostley was great in the sketch and Ronny Graham played the kid who wouldn't listen to the father. I just turned it upside down. The father was a pickpocket and wanted his son to be a criminal . . . and a good criminal, and good at his job. But he kept being "good." That was the switch. The kid couldn't go bad. And finally, the key to the comedy is Paul Lynde [as the father] asks Ronny Graham for his report card, hoping he'd get C's and F's, and he picks it up and he says, "A? . . . A??!!! . . . " and the A's get louder and bigger until he screams in tears and goes offstage crying "A?!!!! A??!!!!" And there's this silence for a long time and then Alice Ghostley playing Mildred Dunnock turns to her son and says, "You're killing that man." That was the biggest laugh in all of the '52 *New Faces*.

That was the reference, the reference was *Death of a Salesman*, and what to point out and how to have fun with it. I'll tell ya', a sketch, if it's a good sketch, should have a beginning, a middle, and an end, and it should have tremendous references that the audience really knows, so that you don't have to work hard getting the laughs. You just have to have fun with the clichés that are already there.

What really made Dunlap a baller is that he actually described *Darby's Return* as a comic sketch. Yes, a comic sketch. And as far as I am aware, this is the first time where a comedic performance was ever officially referred to as a sketch.

As years went by, legit theaters would give these acts names, and they would list them on what was basically the great-great-grandfather of the playbill, something called a card.

And there were lots of different kinds of acts too. They could include anything from jugglers to singers to acrobats . . . and all of this entertainment would be served up before you got to the main theatrical offering— which was at the time most likely a three-act or five-act drama or tragedy.

The term *variety* was used in the 1850s to describe a show that was composed of *just* these short little acts . . . just the double stuff, if you will. So, no need to stick around for that emotionally draining three-hour play, as there wasn't one.

Even right now, if you really didn't want to, you don't actually have to sit through all of a pesky basketball game (which I personally could do every day forever). But *someone else* might not want to do that, and instead turn on the TV and watch an entire show just about cheerleaders.

Or, instead of watching an entire sitcom waiting for that cute three-year-old on the screen to say something clever, you can now watch an entire show about adorable toddlers and the darndest things they say. That's something you can do. That is out there. You could probably even watch an entire show about toddler cheerleaders. I mean why not. That's a good idea. Maybe there should be a toddler-cheerleader show. Um . . . *Cheer Kids*, *Cheer Babies*, *Beer Leaders*, *Beer Chattels*, *Cheadlers*. Yes, *Cheadlers*. And then maybe Don Cheadle can host it. That could work.

Where was I? Variety, and back to the 1800s, where audiences can't get enough of variety shows. How could they not? Bears bouncing on balls, dance numbers, and . . . my favorite part: dun, dun, dahhhhh . . . the sketch.

These early sketches usually took the form of shortened versions of popular tragedies of the time. Then someone brilliantly decided to make them short *and* funny.

For example, a variety show version of *Hamlet* could go something like this,

> *My dad's dead. I'm sad. I think my uncle did it. I want revenge. I say a lot of stuff. My girlfriend's dead. I'm angry. Sword fight. Everybody is dead. I'm dead too . . . Wait, if I'm dead, how am I still talking?*

Today, it would be like doing the short version of *The Sixth Sense* where only a few minutes into the performance a kid says,

> *I see dead people . . . and you're one of them.*

And no, I'm not apologizing, as I'm taking the stance that I can't spoil the same movie twice. And y'all really should have seen that movie by now.

Or, if they were making a parody of *Sophie's Choice*, they would knock it down from like two hours to just the scene where she . . . uh . . . chooses . . . does she choose? Is that the thing that she does? I know there's a choice that's super important and like about life and death maybe . . . Okay. I really should have seen that movie by now. That's on me. Hey pot, I'm the kettle.

Anyhow, this wacky whittled-down world of variety expanded and transformed. Variety became an umbrella that grew to cover different categories of entertainment such as British music hall, minstrelsy, burlesque, vaudeville, and the Broadway revue (also known simply as revue).

These next levels of variety entertainment became a little more structured and organized. To start, in the 1830s and 1840s, small pubs around England would have evenings with, you guessed it, a *variety* of different entertainments. It was mostly dancing, singing, and sing-alongs, but there were also sketches that would be performed as part of the evening. This

> *Today, it would be like doing the short version of* The Sixth Sense *where only a few minutes into the performance a kid says,* I see dead people . . . and you're one of them.

new and improved evening of entertainment was known as "British music hall."

And even though they called it British music hall, it didn't mean a specific place. It referred to the *type* of event. So, for example, a friend could ask you,

What are you doing on Friday night?

And you would tell them,

Well, my good fellow, I'm going to British music hall.

In today's world, it would be something like saying,

How 'bout later we hit some karaoke, bruh.

British music hall created a bit of a stir with the local leaders and people actually had to pay a fee to get into the music hall business. At one point there was even a law on the books that prohibited you from performing a sketch during a music hall show without filing for the proper license.

But thankfully, a lot of the bars and pubs just did it on the sly. Now, I know you may be thinking: Breaking a law if you perform comedy? That's absurd, preposterous, and, well, not very funny at all.

We could make fun of the Brits for this, but we really don't have a leg to stand on. I mean if anyone is up for going down a strange laws in entertainment *in America* rabbit hole, here we are over a hundred years later, and in this corner . . .

In the great state of Indiana anyone with a puppet show, wire dancing, or tumbling act must pay a $3 fine.

Coming in at three pounds two ounces is the minimum amount of clothing a woman must wear in Helena, Montana, to be able to dance on a bar.

And from North Dakota . . . we have way too many to count . . . but to give you a taste, it's against the law to lie down and fall asleep with your shoes on.

And in Fargo, it's illegal to dance while wearing a hat.

I'm not sure where that leaves yarmulkes and the "Hava Nagila" at little Benjamin's bar mitzvah, but at least the rabbi can still legally tell a joke.
And he will.
Ooh . . . he will.
Should I? Yeah, why not . . .
Okay, Rabbi. Let's hear what you got, old man.

Thank you, Keegelah.

You hear the one about the old lady who yells downstairs to her husband? She says, "Morty, why don't you come upstairs and make love to me?"

And he says, "Fine . . .

. . . but I can't do both."

Ha, ha, ha, I can't do both.

Mazel tov, Benjamin!

Now, since we're being a little inappropriate anyway, this may be a good time to share our next form of variety. Round about when music hall was hitting its height, across the pond in the United States, a controversial type of entertainment became very popular. It was called "minstrelsy." Minstrelsy predates both burlesque and vaudeville.

Many of the minstrel shows performed in that era were unfortunately done in something called *blackface*. Yes, blackface. And if you don't know what that is, it's where non-Black performers would apply burnt cork or greasepaint to their faces to give the appearance of being Black.

And no, I don't understand it. It's kind of like these white women today who get cornrows and spray tans and they go on Instagram and y'all can't tell who's a sister and who isn't. It just doesn't make any sense to me.

At any rate, a minstrel show had a few parts to it. The first act usually had something known as the *Tambo and Bones*. Two, sometimes three, performers would play songs written for tambourine and banjo. They would stop in the middle of their performance to tell a couple of topical jokes and then resume the music. The second act was called *the olio* and was a collection of different acts from the troupe at large, like piano playing and dancing, acrobatics, or tumbling, et cetera. A third act could be a parody of some piece of a longer dramatic play or a book.

They would often give these parodies (or *burlesques*) humorous titles from classic works from folks like Shakespeare, with funny names like *Hamlet the Dainty* and *Julius Sneezer*. These early forms of sketches were usually pretty lengthy, and longer than the other styles I'm going to mention. The topic or subject matter was extremely varied and could range from the poignant to the absurd.

There were also Black minstrel shows. Black performers were the true delineators of the art form, seeing as they were *actually* Black. But get this: there's a strange phenomenon during this era where Black minstrels would *also* apply blackface and ostensibly pass for white people—who were pretending to be Black people. I can't even. Ah, the history of America . . . let's go with complicated.

Minstrelsy wasn't the brightest moment in sketch history as it contributed to and reinforced negative Black stereotypes. And although you probably wouldn't be shocked to know that I'm not a fan of this aspect of sketch, it is still an integral step along the way in the development of the art form.

In the 1954 film *White Christmas* with Bing Crosby, Danny Kaye, and Rosemary Clooney, there is a minstrel sketch right smack in the middle of the movie. It was innovative at the time because it was executed *without* blackface. Thankfully, this scene had no whites in blackface and no Blacks in blackface.

Now, when one hears the word *burlesque*, they usually think of acrobatic women swinging from the ceiling in fishnets (and not much else), but

Christopher Guest

MUSIC HALL

Music hall and vaudeville were over seventy-five years ago, essentially. But I believe they still had it in London, even into the '70s. I remember, we would take an ocean liner across with the family and then you land and you take the train in to London. And getting out at Victoria, I remember coming out of the station, and looking up across the way was this huge sort of painted billboard that was on the side of the building. It was called the "The Black and White Minstrel Show." And I remember looking up at this as a kid thinking, *What the hell? What is that?* It seems like something from the 1920s. But they were still doing minstrel shows live in London into the '70s where someone thought: *Well, here's a good idea. We will do this kind of comedy, and enough people will come to see it.* And their music hall stuff you can see on YouTube.

When I did *Family Tree* and we shot in London, I went to some of the old places that were music halls, because we created our own fake music hall sketches. Chris O'Dowd, his family were involved in that, in the fiction of it. But this minstrel thing was still going on. And music hall was different than vaudeville, it had its own subtle differences, I mean, I know about all this stuff, but obviously, I didn't see it. It was mostly over by the 1930s. I'm not that old. Norman Lear is now a hundred . . . Norman may have.

that's certainly not how it started. Originally, if you were *burlesquing* something, you were *parodying* it. Burlesque shows were made up of parodies of higher forms of theater—Shakespeare plays and operas and classic Greek and Roman stories. At least at the time, it was good, clean, sophisticated fun.

Burlesque came into its own in the 1860s when someone decided to write a parody of a Greek myth. They called this burlesque *Ixion; or, The Man at the Wheel.* And this particular show had a very, very scintillating scene with a lady's bare leg. And before you knew it, no more good *clean* fun. Still sophisticated, just not clean. As a matter of fact, these shows became more and more risqué as time went on. It wasn't long before the entertainment was only suitable for adults.

One of my favorite innovations in burlesque is something known as a blackout. A blackout is a very short scene where the performers are ostensibly acting out a joke. Back then, the form was to do a series of five or six of these in succession. The lights would go down, then they would come up on one specific part of the stage and there'd be two people, a man and a woman. As an example, the man would say to the woman,

Why don't you get rid of that fat ass of yours?

And then the woman would respond with,

Well, then there would be no one around here to pay the bills.

THE HISTORY OF SKETCH COMEDY

And blackout.

Then the lights go up on another part of the stage with two other actors.

> MAN #2
>
> My sister-in-law thinks "lettuce" is a proposition.

> WOMAN #2
>
> She never married, did she?

> MAN #2
>
> No, her children wouldn't let her.

Blackout.

> WOMAN #3
>
> Someone is fooling with my knee.

> MAN #3
>
> It's me, and I'm not fooling.

Then another blackout.

It wasn't one comedian telling a joke directly to the audience (like in a stand-up routine). It was usually two or more people interacting and dramatizing a joke.

The comedy school and performance center The Second City uses blackouts quite a bit. One of my favorite blackouts of all time took place on their main stage in the 1960s. A comedian named Lenny Bruce had recently been arrested for using profanity during his act in San Francisco, and it was a really, really big deal at the time. And the blackout I love was set up something like this . . . There was a performer at Second City who was addressing the audience, and he's just kind of just doing patter, saying,

Ladies and gentlemen, welcome to The Second City. You know, here at the show, we . . . blah, blah, blah . . .

And then another actor comes out on the stage and he goes up to the first guy with some alacrity and says,

Hey, did you hear that Lenny Bruce just got busted in San Francisco for profanity?

And then the other guy looks back at him and says,

No shit.

Blackout.

So to tell the story of being shocked about someone cursing onstage, the response was to swear onstage, which I thought was brilliant.

The blackout was a form of comedy that made burlesque unique. And it's pretty much the shortest possible type of scene you can have, and it's a really great one.

The next chapter in variety entertainment is called vaudeville. Vaudeville appeared on burlesque's heels. It started with your standard acts like the bears balancing on balls and the dogs jumping through hoops, a guy who could throw his voice, a lady singing opera—that kind of thing. Then eventually, they started to add some burlesque-esque scenes into the mix.

And where burlesque started to go low, vaudeville went high. Typically, a vaudeville sketch would be longer than a burlesque sketch. I mean, pretty much everything is longer than a blackout, but these new sketches were long. Not the three- to five-minute light comic scenes we see today. Oh no, some of the vaudeville sketches were upwards of fifteen to twenty minutes in length.

You see, back in the day, attention spans, well, they . . . existed. I mean, you're talking about twenty minutes? Hey, even I'm guilty of it. If I go to watch a sketch right now, I'm telling you, you got maybe twenty *seconds* to grab me before I'm checking my phone for football scores, and I'm a human being who LOVES sketch.

Some of these vaudevillian performances were highly physical, like in the comedy act The Three Keatons (featuring a young Buster Keaton—the legendary silent movie actor—and his parents). Other performances were more dramatic and theatrical, like the offerings from the Lunt family. This acting team was composed of Alfred Lunt and his wife, Lynn Fontanne. Together they would perform in plays and vaudeville shows and were a very popular duo. There is a theater on Broadway today called the Lunt-Fontanne, which I am going to assume is named after them, or is an extraordinary coincidence. All in all, the goal of vaudeville was to bring to the world some more family-friendly content.

Of course I'd also like to recognize the Black vaudevillians who contributed their genius to this era. Some of the mainstream vaudeville theaters had maybe only one act per show that would feature African American talent (if that), so it was difficult for them to get exposure in the major vaudeville circuits. And this is truly a shame, because some of the greatest contributions to sketch came from these amazing and creative artists.

There were, however, opportunities for our brothers and sisters to shine on what was known as the T.O.B.A. circuit.

T.O.B.A. stands for Theater Owners Booking Association. But, among Black performers, it stood for "Tough on Black Asses." And even though this sounds like a joke, trust me, it wasn't. My talented brothers and sisters had to sleep on trains, would get shortchanged when getting paid, and most of the time they couldn't even stay in the town in which they were performing because of the color of their skin. Some of the greatest comedic performers of that, or any, era worked the T.O.B.A. circuit—

> *T.O.B.A. stands for Theater Owners Booking Association. But, among Black performers, it stood for "Tough on Black Asses."*

including the likes of Pigmeat Markham, Moms Mabley, Bert Williams, and Sammy Davis Jr.

One great offering to the landscape of sketch from the Black community is what's known as *indefinite talk*. This concept was put on the map by two gentlemen named Flournoy Miller and Aubrey Lyles. Here's an example:

I'm going to take you and your girl out for a ride sometime.

LYLES

Well, that'd be great, man. Can you make it next—

MILLER

Oh no, I'm busy then.

LYLES

Okay. Well, when can you make it?

MILLER

Let's see, the best day for me would be—

LYLES

That suits me. What hour?

MILLER

Anytime between—

LYLES

Oh, that's a bit early, but we'll be there.

It demands a superb grasp of timing and rhythm. Two other gentlemen who helped popularize the indefinite talk form are Mantan Moreland and Ben Carter. Moreland used to work with Aubrey Lyles as well, and he's extremely proficient at this type of scene. There's a really fun bit with Moreland and the uber-dynamic Nipsey Russell:

MORELAND

What kind of races do you play?

RUSSELL

Horse races.

MORELAND

What track you play at?

                         RUSSELL
    Well, I play over there—

                         MORELAND
    That track's crooked.

                         RUSSELL
    Why don't you play over here around—

                         MORELAND
    That's where I lost my money.

                         RUSSELL
    How much did you lose?

                         MORELAND
    Ah, I lost about—

                         RUSSELL
    You didn't have that much.

This is also a good time to highlight the work of Bert Williams. Bert Williams started his career in 1893, and by 1910 he was one of the most respected comedians, Black or white, on the American stage. In the 1919 Follies, there was a shoe store bit that I just love where the clerk asks Bert,

What size do you wear?

And Bert responds,

Well, I wear tens, but the elevens feel so good . . . I wear twelves.

If jokes had sizes, this one would be a size twelve.

One of the greatest pieces of work Bert Williams performed was a routine called *The Poker Game*. It's a wonderful short film where he gets busted at an illegal poker game and he's

If jokes had sizes, this one would be a size twelve.

Moms Mabley began her career by singing and dancing in local shows in Cleveland, Ohio. Eventually, she began to travel the vaudeville circuit and she took the challenges and racism she faced and channeled them into her humor. She stood out for her floppy hats and colorful wardrobe, both met in kind by her colorful Grandma-inspired character. In the 1960s she was working as a stand-up comic and was the first woman comic to play the Apollo theater and Carnegie Hall. It's not surprising that she was an inspiration to many legends such as Eddie Murphy, Whoopie Goldberg, and Richard Pryor. She was also the first openly gay comedian.

sentenced to ten days in jail. And as he sits in his cell alone, he comes up with a way to pass the time by playing poker with a few imaginary friends. The next few minutes are sublime, as he skillfully pantomimes everything that could transpire in a poker game.

The highlight of the routine is right after he's dealt the cards. He asks each one of the other imaginary players how many cards they'd like. And we know from his pantomime that the first guy asks for three cards. Of course, this pleases him and Bert grins this very huge self-satisfied grin. The second guy asks for one card, so Bert looks at him with some mild disappointment. Then the third player requests no cards and Bert's expression quickly turns to that of great concern.

All of his reactions are an absolute master class. He's so specific you can almost see the other men in the room.

I'm making the faces right now. I'm doing it.

No cards . . . ? Uh-oh.

Or maybe instead of trying to imagine Bert, or my face, you could try to find the video: Bert Williams, *The Poker Game*. Masterful.

Our final category is the Broadway revue. Now, Broadway revues were the crème de la crème of variety shows. They had amazing and extravagant production values and massive casts. At the end of the day, a revue was a vaudeville show dressed up in a top hat and tails.

The most well-known purveyor of these types of shows was Flo Ziegfeld, who was the creator and producer of the Ziegfeld Follies. Many of our favorite comedy royals starred in the Follies—people like W. C. Fields, Will Rogers, and Bob Hope.

From around 1916 to 1932 the Broadway revue had its Golden Age. There were acts of all different sizes and scopes and they were wicked popular. During the course of the 1920s, there were close to 150 revues on Broadway. There weren't just sketches, there was music as well. And with all of the opportunities for young performers to hone their craft and be seen, it's not surprising that this is also where composers such as Arthur Schwartz and Irving Berlin got their start.

There were some pretty incredible Black revues as well. In the 1930s, Fats Waller wrote a revue called *Hot Chocolates*. Over time, it moved from Harlem to Broadway and featured the musical genius of both Louis Armstrong and Cab Calloway in the orchestra pit. I personally would have given just about anything to have been there in person to hear them play and to watch the great Fats Waller sing "Ain't Misbehavin'."

Girlfriend Village

Okay, so maybe it wasn't quite the Ziegfeld Follies or Broadway, but back when I was in school in Detroit, a woman I knew asked me to join a troupe that she was putting together. She even had a space for us to perform in (which in the world of theater is a rare and miraculous thing). The name of the show was *Girlfriend Village and Company*. It was an homage to Greenfield Village, one of those interactive historical people in period costume places where folks pretend it's the early 1900s and they teach you how to do things like churn butter.

In the revue, we would perform comedic sketches, sing songs, and play improv games with the audience. The singing was something that set this show apart from your standard sketch show . . . and I guess you could say, set me apart from some of my castmates. It's one thing to be able to improvise, but to improvise a scene and at the same time *also* improvise a melody, is something I was able to excel at.

On *Key & Peele* and many modern sketch and variety shows, actors who excel seem to be those who are able to wear many hats. Also, with the internet and the unlimited access to mountains of content, it appears like there's no limit to the amount of folks who can sing, while playing an instrument, and at the same time also juggle (or be able to do whatever TikTok skill is popular this week). As for me, I can sing and even juggle a little. And although I can't play any instruments, I have been known to shred some stellar air guitar. It's something I picked up in my Renaissance festival days, but back then we called it air lute . . . But more importantly, I picked up a musical improv songwriting skill at *Girlfriend Village*, and have enjoyed making up lyrics on the fly ever since.

Hey You Can't Do That

I do have a variety-themed *Hey You Can't Do That* moment that I am excited to share with you. This moment comes to us thanks to an entertainer named Timmie Rogers. Timmie was an early American television performer and a pioneer in the Black comedy world. He went from being an eight-year-old boy dancing on the streets of Detroit busking for change, to performing at the Apollo Theater in Harlem and opening for Nat King Cole.

In the 1950s, he was one of, if not *the* first African American to put on a tux and step out onstage and perform in front of a white audience. He's also the first Black comedian to have a gold album, and his photo hangs in the Comedy Hall of Fame next to legends like Jack Benny, Milton Berle, and Richard Pryor.

It was at the Apollo, at a show in 1949, that Timmie Rogers first used his catchphrase.

What is his catchphrase, you ask?

It is well . . . something special.

Oh Yeeeah!

Yes, that's it.

That's all of it. That's the whole thing.

Oh Yeeeah!

And he says it after almost every line. And I mean like almost every line. After every *good* joke,

Oh Yeeeah!

and sadly, after every *not so good* joke,

Oh Yeeeah!

And ol' Timmie's stage routine went a little something like this:

Money, money, money, money. Everybody want money. And you know money is the root of all evil . . .

and I'm trying to find those roots.

Oh Yeeeah!

People like Bing Crosby, the Vanderbilts, the Rockefellers, Bob Hope, Ella Fitzgerald, you think they're happy?

Oh Yeeeah!

But, they have their problems, because the more money they make, the more taxes they got to pay. They in a very high tax bracket. Now, I was home last night trying to figure out my taxes for this year. And after I figured it out, I got two words to say to you.

I'm broke.

Oh Yeeeah!

You see this suit? Three years old.

You see the pockets? Brand new.

Oh Yeeeah!

It's sooo good.

And they have a new kind of tax plan now where they ask you three questions. How much did you make? Where is it at? Send it.

They have what they call an estimated tax plan too. Then you got to guess how much you're going to make, figure it out, sign it, and send it in.

Well, I sent mine in too, but I didn't sign it. No! I figured if I have to guess how much I'm going to make . . . let them guess who sent it in.

And they did.

Oh Yeeeah!

Oh Yeeeah! I know what y'all might be thinking, but I'm not pulling your leg. Look it up, Timmie Rogers. Look that shit up. And for me, I like to imagine that this is like how he talks all the time. Like, anywhere, just going through his day . . . excuse me, sir, would you like to see the menu? *Oh Yeeeah!* Can I give you a lift to the airport, Timmie? *Oh Yeeeah!*

So if you're thinking, hey, ain't nobody can do that, you can't just use "Oh Yeeeah!" as your catchphrase, I'm telling you, *Oh Yeeeah* you can!

And Timmie starts and ends his show with a song where the words of the chorus are:

Everybody wants to go to heaven, but nobody wants to die.

Fortunately for Timmie, it was the crowd who was dying . . . of laughter.

Oh Yeeeah!

CHAPTER 4

A Face for Radio

In 1897, a man named Tesla filed a basic radio patent application. Around the same time another gentleman by the name of Marconi was also credited for the origins of the radio. Now, it's 100 percent above my pay grade to decide *exactly* who was responsible and for what . . . but something I do know is that radio changed how we communicate and gave the world a new way to get entertainment to the masses.

Although it started as an invaluable tool for communication with ships at sea, pilots, truck drivers, and law enforcement, the radio soon became extremely accessible to everyone else. Whether it was to hear the news of the world or to enjoy rural barn and dance programs (which I'm guessing is just what it sounds like), folks began to flock to this new exciting medium.

Purchasing a radio during the Great Depression was perhaps too big an investment for many folks at the time, but by the end of the 1930s, 40 percent of the United States (about twelve million households) owned a radio. Of course, once corporations saw that there was potential to make money with this new invention, there was no turning back.

Comedy entertainment found itself a new home as well. As radio began growing in popularity, jokes and sketches, and the folks who performed them, found their own path from the stage . . . not to the screen, but to the microphone.

As you can imagine, some comedians and their acts could translate more easily to radio than others. When it comes to vaudeville and burlesque, sure, there were a *variety* of comedy acts, but most of them had humor that was visual. Many of the early stage comedians were kings and queens of slapstick and physical comedy, and of course, a whole lotta lazzi.

The acts and actors who made the most seamless transition were the early sketch vaudevillians who had spent years creating and performing in parodies. They knew how to write an elaborate scene or scenario by providing the audience with detailed exposition. They were joined by the joke tellers and the comedic performers who were adept at turns of phrase and traditional jokes. By "traditional" I'm referring to the ones that had setups and punch lines, and jokes that didn't need any costumes or complicated backdrops to get a laugh from their audience.

As sponsors were demanding content, it was our favorite wordsmith comics who rose to the top. If someone's "A" material was based on *visual* gags, or funny facial expressions, it was harder for them to adapt to this new medium. Folks did their best to repurpose whatever material they could from their vaudeville and burlesque acts to the radio.

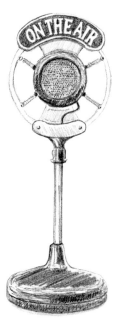

George Burns and Gracie Allen were a married comedy team who thrived on the stage. Their jokes, and Gracie Allen's ditzy onstage persona, were developed in the laboratory known as vaudeville—tested night after night and perfected by trial and error. And luckily for them, because their humor was built on their witty banter and verbal interactions, they appeared to make the transition to radio seamlessly. It's easy to see how popular they became

with performances like this one . . .

                              BURNS

    Do you like to love?

                              ALLEN

    No.

                              BURNS

    Like to kiss?

                              ALLEN

    No.

                              BURNS

    What do you like?

                              ALLEN

    Lamb chops.

                              BURNS

    Lamb chops. Could you eat two big lamb chops alone?

Alone? Oh, no, not alone . . .

with potatoes I could.

We can delight in Burns and Allen and their witty plays on words without the visuals of a fancy set and everything that goes with it.

There were a number of folks who headed out into this new frontier, and it wasn't long before their most popular stage bits could be heard on the radio.

For example, there's an old vaudeville routine by the comedy team of Weber and Fields. This sketch was something they did together on a stage. Years later on the radio there was a very popular routine performed by another comedy duo that was perhaps *inspired* by the deft wordplay of Weber and Fields in the scene below.

See if you can figure out *who* and *what* I'm referring to . . .

WEBER

Oh, I'm zo happy to see you. Vat are ya doing downtown here?

FIELDS

Vell, I verk here.

WEBER

You verk around here?

FIELDS

Yes, I do.

WEBER

Oh zat's vonderful, because you are the only one zat doesn't make me nervous. Vhy don't you haff lunch vis me zometime?

FIELDS

I'd love to.

WEBER

I'll tell you vot I'll do. If you tell me the name of the street vhere you are, I'll come pick you up.

FIELDS

Vut Street.

WEBER

The street you verk on so I come pick you up.

FIELDS

Vut Street.

WEBER

The street you're verking on.

FIELDS

Vut Street.

WEBER

The street where you verk.

FIELDS

Vut Street!

WEBER

I'm asking you! Don't you ask me! Now tell me the street. Everything has a name. The city has a name. You have a name. Now vut is the name of the street you verk on?!

FIELDS

Calm down. Look, I verk on Vut Street. I'll shpell it for you, okay?

W-A-T-T.

Vut Street, see?

WEBER

Oh, Vatt Street! Vy didn't you say zo! I thought you were making fun of me.

They performed this sketch many years before radio came on the scene, and because of the tradition of passing down bits, it's certainly possible this word game was the influence for one of the greatest radio routines of all time. And, when it comes to the routine I'm referring to, *What* wasn't the name of the street; instead, it was the name of the player on second base.

Abbott and Costello's *Who's on First* works in the same tradition as the sketch known as *Watt Street*; they both use a brilliant combination of wordplay and misunderstanding. Thankfully, humor based on misunderstanding is just as popular today as it was a hundred years ago. Think about it: without comedy based on mix-ups and misinterpretations, there wouldn't have been eight seasons of *Three's Company* . . . we wouldn't have fallen in love with a bartender on *Cheers* named Coach . . .

Without comedy based on mix-ups and misinterpretations, there wouldn't have been eight seasons of Three's Company.

and Gilligan and his island buddies would certainly have been rescued like, I dunno . . . four hundred times.

The bigger point is that vaudeville was a fertile training ground and a resource for radio artists. Many performers had spent years perfecting their routines on a stage before this opportunity to bring their material to airways presented itself. It seems vaudevillian comedic performers had been training for an opportunity that they didn't even know was coming.

One of those multifaceted performers was a gentleman by the name of Bob Hope. Bob Hope's calling card was playing a wisecracker who would tell strong, funny jokes. As part of the format on his radio show, Bob would regularly introduce a guest and then chat with them, and this banter would be based on scripted jokes. But they would rattle off this witty banter casually, as if they were just talking. This kind of chat is known as cross talk or patter. That bit I shared earlier from Burns and Allen also falls under the category of cross talk. In a cross talk, usually there's one person who sets up the jokes, and the other who knocks them down.

When it came to Bob Hope and his guests, very often after a few minutes of patter, Bob would use the end of their conversation as a segue into a sketch. For example, he had Rita Hayworth on his show. After their initial chat, Rita casually mentioned that she went to a farm and met *the cutest farm boy*. This was the setup. From here, the sound on their casual conversation faded, and Rita and Bob started a sketch . . .

                         RITA
    Yoohoo. Hello there?

                         BOB
                 [In a country twang]
    Howdy, ma'am. Are you a gal from the city?

                         RITA
    Yes.

                         BOB
    Well, my ma warned me about gals from the city.

                         RITA
    She did?

                         BOB
    Yeah, but Ma ain't around . . .
    So come on in.

This kind of performance was super innovative. Even though it aired as part of a radio show, you can tell that instead of the two of them standing on the stage as themselves and participating in traditional cross talking and joke telling, Bob and Rita created characters and did their cross talk inside the confines of a sketch, in this case on the farm. It was with radio sketches like this one where we can see the clear beginnings of something known as a situation comedy. And these *situational comedies*

These situational comedies *were the next important step on the path to what we call* sitcoms *today.*

were the next important step on the path to what we call *sitcoms* today.

On a vaudeville stage, comedians didn't have to contend with the limitations imposed by working on the radio, or by parameters set by radio show sponsors. When it came to fitting in to this new medium (with its limitations on formats and running time), having serialized and recognizable characters and plots gave the creators the luxury to not have to start from scratch with every show. Fans of a show were able to get on board with very little setup. Using this format, the performers could jump right into the meat of the story line. It's a whole lot easier when the audience already knows who is the bad guy, who is the dope, and who is the voice of reason. (I see you trying, Professor, but as smart as we know you are, y'all still ain't getting off that island.)

Anyway, when it came to radio, folks like Bob Hope and others went back to our commedia roots and took advantage of the benefits of creating comedy from recognizable and recurring characters and relationships, and they did it with aplomb.

A great example of something being *situational* would be a James Bond movie. Everyone knows who Bond . . . James Bond, is. We know what to expect from him in every situation. We even know how he likes his martinis. See what I mean? No real backstory is needed for each new adventure and you can just get right into the explosions, the lovemaking, and the car chases. And for over sixty years, audiences, including myself, haven't been able to get enough of it. Well, except for maybe *Octopussy* though. There was a movie called *Octopussy*. I mean, what the heck is that? I mean, just right there on the poster, there's just a picture of a woman and above it was the word *Octopussy*, just like on a poster out there in the front of the movie theater. Kids walking by like it's no big deal. Anyway, that one someone needs to explain to me. *The Spy Who Loved Me*? I'm good. *Casino Royale*? Good too. *Octopussy*? No idea what that is. But thankfully I do know what to expect from 007 when the lights go down and the music starts.

S l o w . . . Talkers

One of my favorite comedy teams to do sketch on the radio is Bob and Ray. The team of Bob and Ray was made up of Bob Elliott and Ray Goulding. They had their share of recurring characters, but their bread and butter were sketches that followed similar and simple setups and themes. My favorite of these were their mock radio news programs and public interest pieces.

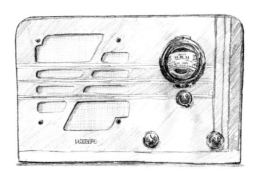

This kind of banter worked very well within the radio format. They were played very straight (meaning realistic and dry), so if you were only half listening, their routines could easily be mistaken for actual interviews . . . except they were anything but. These pieces usually sounded like one real guy talking to another real guy on the radio.

One of my favorite sketches of theirs is called *Slow Talkers of America*. This sketch starts fairly harmlessly with Ray Goulding asking Bob,

RAY

Would you tell us your name and where you're from, sir?

BOB

Arlow . . . . . P . . . . . Whitcomb . . . . .
from . . . . . Glens Falls . . . . .

RAY

[Finishing Bob's sentence for him]

New York? Glens Falls, New York?

BOB

. . . . . New . . . . . York. I am . . . . .
the . . . . . president . . . . . and . . . . .
recording . . . . .

RAY

Secretary?

                                  BOB
    . . . . . secretary . . . . .

So, okay, at this point Ray Goulding (who's playing the interviewer) is having a real hard time because he pretty much knows what the end of the sentence is going to be. And I mean, I get it. I have a hard time not interrupting people who are talking at *regular* speed. So, my man is just trying so hard to be polite, but also like, let's get on with it, brother. Let's get on with it, you know? Then Bob continues,

    . . . . . secretary . . . . . of . . . . .
    the . . . . . S . . . . . T . . . . .
    O . . . . . A . . . . .

And then Ray's like,

    What's that stand for? The Slow Talkers of America,
    right? America? America??!

My man then says slow talkers of America, SLOWLY. That's my jam, or maybe more appropriately, my molasses. And by now, Ray Goulding's done. He's finished. He's freakin' done. This is just not working for him, but he can't just get up and leave, he's got to finish the interview, right? So here we go again,

                                  BOB
    We . . . . . believe . . . . . in . . . . .
    forming . . . . . our . . . . .
    thoughts . . . . . ideas . . . . .
    and . . . . . opinions . . . . . thoroughly.

                                  RAY
    Before speaking so you'll never be misunderstood,
    right?!!

                                  BOB
    Before . . . . . uttering . . . . .

                                  RAY
    So, you'll never be misunderstood!!?!?!?

                              BOB

So . . . . . that . . . . . we . . . . .
will . . . . . never . . . . . be . . . . .
misunderstood. We . . . . . are . . . . .
here . . . . . in . . . . . Los Angeles,
attending . . . . . our . . . . .
annual . . . . .

                              RAY

Convention!?!?! Your annual convention! You're here
for your annual convention?!????

                              BOB

. . . . . mem . . . . . ber . . . . . ship

                              RAY

Convention!!!?? Convention!!!

                              BOB

. . . . . convention. All . . . . .
two . . . . . hundred . . . . .

                              RAY

Members??!?! Members!!

                              BOB

. . . . . and . . . . . fif-ty . . . . .

                              RAY

Members!!!!

                              BOB

. . . . . seven . . . . .

                              RAY

Members!!??!?!?

                              BOB

. . . . . members.

What really gets me is the "game." The scene works so well because of the game that was set up: an *impatient* man having to be *extraordinarily patient.* But, the best part of the scene for me is when they add another layer to their comedic game, and this happens when Ray tries guessing what Bob's going to say. And even *that* evolves. In the beginning Ray was correct at what he thought was coming, but then Bob starts saying different words than Ray's confident callouts.

Sure, at the end of "*Slow Talkers of America,*" you know he's going to say "*America.*" But when my man says "*before speaking, so you'll never be misunderstood?*" and Bob says "*before uttering,*" that really got me.

I find this shit hilarious. And I love that it's rolled up in a brilliant and simple sketch. Hopefully you're still with me on this one. I just love Bob and Ray, mostly because I just never

. . . . . heard . . . . . anything . . . . . like . . . . . that . . . . .

Before!?!?!?

. . . . . before.

It's just good. This is good. This is so good. Oh man. Bob and Ray were so imaginative and the sketches they did felt so real. The dry, the deadpan, and the casual sincerity they brought to their work was something fresh and new.

And it predated, by the way, the mockumentary style of comedy that was later made popular by performers such as Ricky Gervais and Christopher Guest. But most importantly, for our purposes . . . . . it . . . . . was . . . . . stellar . . . . . sketch . . . . .

COMEDY!!??!

. . . . . comedy.

Ken Jeong

SHORT AMOUNT OF TIME

There is something about the self-containment of sketches, and that you have to get across a story in five minutes. You know, how do you get a beginning, a middle, and an end. It's hard, and it's a lot harder than people give it credit for. When you're doing a movie or an episodic show you have a bit of time to tell that story. And even then, sometimes it's not long enough. But in sketch you have this absurdly short amount of time to get across a story with a beginning, a middle, and an end. And you know it's a testament to the writers and the comedians that participate in that. I'm always in awe of *SNL*, and all the great sketch shows.

Julia Louis-Dreyfus

THE MUSCLE I RELY ON THE MOST

What I was drawn to was ensemble comedy. I mean, I just loved it. Mary Tyler Moore, Carol Burnett, Dick Van Dyke, the very beginning of *Saturday Night Live*; all of that stuff where you could see people working in tandem and with each other very well. Those shows were all ensemble comedy shows, and there is a relationship between ensemble work and sketch comedy. Sketch comedy informed me as an *actor*. So, everything I took away from sketch comedy, as it were—which is really *ensemble work and thinking on your feet,* in a sense—I have taken and applied as an actor. And it's been the most valuable tool of my life, to tell you the truth. It's a muscle group that certain actors aren't comfortable with, but it's the only muscle I'm used to. And I think it applies to both writing and acting. Because in some regards, they're one and the same. To a certain extent . . . it's the muscle I rely on the most.

Spoken Word

My first experience of *Saturday Night Live* came from listening to sketches from the show on a cassette tape. And for those of you who don't know what a cassette tape is, ask your grandparents . . . which really hurts me because I know to jump right over your parents. Your parents may not know what it is, but your grandparents for sure know what it is, which makes me really sad, because *I* know what it is. At any rate, I used to listen to a cassette tape titled *The Best of Saturday Night Live*, and on that tape, there were incredible sketches from the original cast of the Not Ready for Primetime Players.

On road trips with my dad and my stepmother, I would listen to these tapes on either a boom box or in the cassette chute in our Vanagon camper. Okay, I just made up that phrase: cassette chute. I'm pretty sure that's not what it's called. But there indeed was a little thing that you would stick cassette tapes into that predated your car's CD player. (Which cars also don't have any more either. Again, ask your grandparents.)

This *Saturday Night Live* cassette was my first foray into hearing spoken word comedy. Prior to this, I had only ever watched comedy in movies and on TV. When I *listened* to comedy, it allowed me to create and generate images in my mind and I delighted in this new process, and soon I was hooked. Hearing comedy helped me appreciate the written word and the skill it takes to write a clever joke. In this art form the comedian can't rely on pratfalls or funny faces, as their words became the most valuable part of their act.

I have always been curious about how to create the perfect comedic show recipe. For example, why does the timing of a song go really well after a twenty-minute monologue? Why were the sketches usually found in the middle of the show?

Putting together the running order of a program is a real art, and a modern

On road trips with my dad and my stepmother, I would listen to these tapes on either a boom box or in the cassette chute in our Vanagon camper. Okay, I just made up that phrase: cassette chute.

sketch show operates a little differently from vaudeville. In vaudeville, they would usually start with a silent act (otherwise known as a dumb show or pantomime), giving stragglers in the audience time to find a seat without stepping on anyone's dialogue. At The Second City, our audience was seated and primed for entertainment at showtime. This way our shows could start with an attention-grabbing group number, some loud music, singing, or dancing. Then, the next scenes or sketches put some of the best material for that show on the stage. We call this "the credential scene" or "three spot," letting the crowd know they're going to be seeing a quality show.

A lot of my education about how to put all of these pieces together came from my early love of spoken word comedy. And as a young man in Detroit, one of my first tastes of a successful running order came from listening to the radio and the words,

A lot of my education about how to put all of these pieces together came from my early love of spoken word comedy.

Well, it was a quiet week in Lake Wobegon.

Growing up in the Midwest, I heard that phrase every weekend when I sat around the radio with my dad and my brother while my stepmother prepared lunch. The program started with a song, and then the host, Garrison Keillor, would tell us who his guests were that week. At some point he would launch into some warm and wonderful yarn about his hometown in Minnesota. For years, I wondered whether Lake Wobegon was real or just a handful of fantastic fictions created for me and the rest of his loyal radio audience.

Every story Keillor shared sounded more real than the last. He wove tales about the local cafe owner, bachelor Lutheran farmers, and other crazy inhabitants of this incredible town on his long-running NPR show: *A Prairie Home Companion.*

Undoubtedly, part of *Prairie Home*'s success was Keillor's genius at mixing and perfecting the order of the elements of his show—variety, music, sketch comedy, storytelling—all for the maximum entertainment impact. Sitting as a family unit and listening intently to the radio was a tradition for many Americans, and for my family, tuning in to *A Prairie Home Companion* every weekend on NPR was, and remains, my most intimate relationship with radio variety shows.

Every week, it was a time to be excited and contemplative. And I couldn't wait to sing the jingle for the fictitious sponsor of *A Prairie Home Companion*, Powder Milk Biscuits. I have consumed quite a lot of spoken word comedy throughout the years, and yes, my journey began with the radio and hearing Garrison Keillor finishing his monologue by saying,

> *Well, that's the news from Lake Wobegon, where all the women are strong, all the men are good looking, and all the children are above average.*

In my childhood, the radio wasn't the only delivery system for spoken word comedy. My parents also had a record player. (Which is making a comeback, and thanks to musicians like Jack White opening record stores, that one I don't need to explain.) Our record player was called an Emerson; it had a giant equalizer with sliders, and sat in the corner of my father and stepmother's townhouse.

This is where I first heard *Whoopi Goldberg: Direct from Broadway*. It's where I sat in awe and glee marveling at the genius of Richard Pryor's *Wanted*. And it was also the place where I discovered the work of one of the greatest comedic soul mate teams of all time, Mike Nichols and Elaine May.

Hey You Can't Do That

For this chapter's *Hey You Can't Do That* moment, I'd like to share one of my favorite spoken word sketches. If anyone reading this has any *#comedyteamcouplesgoals*, I highly recommend that you take some time and study up on any and all things Nichols and May.

The following sketch is called *Morning Rounds*, and in it Mike Nichols plays a doctor checking in on a hospital patient played by Elaine May. He starts with routine medical questions, but soon reveals his agenda may not be what you think . . .

Christopher Guest
THE NATIONAL LAMPOON RADIO HOUR

I was at the *National Lampoon* when it started; I was twenty-two years old. And I wrote an article and they said, "We'll publish this." And I said, "Oh really?" Then I said, "What I really do is sort of spoken comedy, and I play music and I do all these things . . ." They built a studio for us. We made six record albums and we had a radio show. So, me, with John Belushi, and Bill Murray, Brian Murray, Paul Schafer; we did this show. And that was 1973 or something. It was called *The National Lampoon Radio Hour*. I think we did fifty-eight shows. It was a crazy thing and we just did whatever we wanted. We had this state-of-the-art studio, and we would go in there and just do what we did as young, sort of smart-ass people, and it went out over the airwaves. It was on two hundred stations throughout the country. There were people who wrote pieces and we acted in them. The pieces I did, especially with Bill Murray, were all improvised. The music obviously was not, the music we recorded. And they were songs, and different combinations of people wrote the songs. And they let us do whatever we wanted. That was a precursor to what I was going to do later in my career.

                    DR. BLOOM
                    [Softly]

Mrs. Lotke. Mrs. Lotke. This is Dr. Bloom. Can you
hear me, Mrs. Lotke?

                    MRS. LOTKE
                    [Groggy]

Oh, Dr. Bloom . . .

                    DR. BLOOM

How are you feeling?

                    MRS. LOTKE
                 [Groaning noises]

                    DR. BLOOM

Now, have you been awake for the last half hour or so?

                    MRS. LOTKE
              [Trying to get her bearings]

On, on and off . . . I think so . . . I think that the
intravenous slipped out.

                    DR. BLOOM

Oh, we'll take care of that. Look, Mrs. Lotke, has
Nurse Radetzky been in here?

                    MRS. LOTKE

Oh, she was the nurse . . . ?

                    DR. BLOOM

She was tall? Terribly attractive dark nurse?

                    MRS. LOTKE

Oh yeah, yes, no, yes she was. I tried to get her in
here to tell her the intravenous had slipped out. She
said she was busy and . . .

                    DR. BLOOM

But she was in here?

MRS. LOTKE

She was doing something else and she was, she
was . . .

DR. BLOOM

Mrs. Lotke, did she mention me at all?

MRS. LOTKE
[Confused]

What . . . ?

DR. BLOOM

Did she mention me at all?

MRS. LOTKE

Oh, you mean, in what way?

DR. BLOOM

I mean, did she say anything about last night?

MRS. LOTKE

Oh, she said, wait . . . she said, let me, she was
tired or something.

DR. BLOOM

Did she seem tired? She seemed tired? Did she seem
angry or anything?

I mean, once he hears the word *tired*, my man is like, oh, she was,
she was tired? Did she say anything about me? It's just, it's sublime. He
continues digging,

DR. BLOOM

You know the nurse I'm talking about now, Nurse
Radetzky?

MRS. LOTKE

Oh yeah, she was very mad. She was very—

DR. BLOOM

No, no, no, not Ms. Flown. Ms. Flown is the sort of
squat one.

MRS. LOTKE

Oh, I haven't, I haven't had a squat nurse. Just a
tall one.

DR. BLOOM

Yes, that's right, that's Ms. Radetzky, Nurse
Radetzky. Now, did she seem angry? Did she mention my
name? Did she mention anything about . . . ?

MRS. LOTKE

She asked if you had been in here . . .

DR. BLOOM

Oh, she did? She did?

MRS. LOTKE

She asked . . .

<pre>
                         DR. BLOOM
She did? She did?

                         MRS. LOTKE
She asked me . . . if you were here in the . . .

                         DR. BLOOM
Yes, yeah, yeah, yeah?
</pre>

You know what I mean? We've all been there. I mean, you got to, you want to know how the date went, right?

<pre>
                         DR. BLOOM
Yeah. Yeah. She asked if I said anything about her.
Did she?

                         MRS. LOTKE
Oh yeah, yeah.

                         DR. BLOOM
                    [Exits the room]
Oh, she did!

Oh, oh, Mrs. Lotke, you've made me the happiest doctor
on the floor!

                         MRS. LOTKE
               [Confused and calling after him]
Doctor, but my intravenous . . .

                         DR. BLOOM
               [Calling back from hallway]
I'll see you later.

                         MRS. LOTKE
Aren't you going to examine me?

                         DR. BLOOM
Ah, you're okay. Take your temperature.
</pre>

THE HISTORY OF SKETCH COMEDY

Take your temperature. My man said, take your temperature??! He can't do that and just leave the room.

"Take your temperature. You'll be fine."

Wow. My man just left. What about her intravenous?

That's one ballsy-ass doctor. Talkin' 'bout "take your temperature" and he says it while he's already down the hall and in the elevator. Nurse Radetzky? He's gonna find her. She's got to be here somewhere . . .

CHAPTER 5

That's Entertainment?

The comedian Steve Allen once said, "Radio is the theater of the mind. TV is the theater of the mindless." Like most of you, I can't imagine a world without television. I not only grew up as an avid fan of the medium, but it was also on TV that I found my calling, and I'm grateful for every single minute of it.

Now, we know that when it comes to comedy, the people who were successful on radio were the ones who could tell clever, funny jokes or conjure up a vivid image in the listener's mind. So, where did that leave the *physical* comedians? Well, thankfully, many of them found their way to the silver screen and then to television. Physical humor maybe didn't go over so well on the radio waves, but it certainly lent itself to the visual medium of the tube. Folks like Sid Caesar, Milton Berle, Ernie Kovacs, and Jack Benny could tell jokes and *also* were adept at physical bits. These double threats, if you will, did really well for themselves. Bob Hope was also one of these multi-hyphenates. He had a radio show, was in movies, and then also had a television variety show.

In the late 1940s, television started gaining traction, but there was one person who many would argue is responsible for single-handedly turning television into the most popular form of entertainment of the time: Milton Berle.

Milton Berle was another of those powerhouse vaudeville stage performers who moved to radio. When television came along he was given the opportunity to be one of a number of hosts in rotation on a TV show called *Texaco Star Theater*. There were a handful of other hosts on this program who did their job, and they did it well. But when Berle was in the spotlight it was magic. It wasn't long before he became a permanent fixture on the show.

Tuesday nights, within minutes of the show's finale, there was even a marked difference in water usage.

Now, here is something that really bakes my noodle. When *Texaco Star Theater* first premiered, there were about 175,000 television sets in homes across America. But, by the end of just the *first* season of *Texaco Star Theater*, there were—and this is the incredible part—750,000 televisions that were turned on, and tuned in, to see the beloved Uncle Miltie.

Supposedly, on Tuesday nights, within minutes of the show's finale, there was even a marked difference in water usage because that's the moment when everyone finally got up from their TV sets *at the same time* to go to the bathroom. I mean, Milton Berle was it. My man straight up made TV a popular medium. He was, albeit indirectly, like the greatest television salesperson ever. That's badass.

Milton Berle was joined in this new medium by other great performers. An uber-talented fellow by the name of Jack Benny was also given his own show, and he brought some of his characters from his radio program over to TV with him. One of the ingenious and creative things Jack did that set him apart

THE HISTORY OF SKETCH COMEDY

was to create a *persona* for himself as a host—and in this case, someone who was cheap and stingy.

My understanding is that this very specific character choice was inspired by his friend Fred Allen. Fred knew that Jack was listening to his radio show (*The Fred Allen Show*) and on his show, as a joke, he called Jack cheap. So, to keep the bit going, Jack on his own radio show decided that he would pretend to be a penny-pincher as a way to take a dig at Fred. The fans just loved this rivalry. It didn't matter if it was fictional or not. The audiences ate it up. And when Jack moved his show to television, he kept up the act.

Jack did a sketch on his radio show where he's being held up at gunpoint. It went over so well that he created the live version of the same sketch for TV.

> MUGGER
>
> Don't make a move. This is a stickup.
>
> [Beat]
>
> You heard me.
>
> JACK BENNY
>
> Mister, put down that gun.
>
> MUGGER
>
> Now come on. Your money or your life.

But Benny doesn't respond. So, the guy gets angry and tries again.

> MUGGER
>
> Look, bud . . . I SAID YOUR MONEY OR YOUR LIFE.

And Jack Benny sighs and then in the most coy way possible, he muses . . .

> JACK BENNY
>
> I'm thinking it over.

That was his character to a T. And the fake-rivalry bit went over like gangbusters. These bits, they stand the test of time because they work, and when done right, are funny as heck. And although this may seem like an odd comparison, there are some pretty fun Fred Allen and Jack Benny–type rivalries that exist today in the WWE (World Wrestling Entertainment). For example, even though they talk smack about each other in public, Dwayne "The Rock" Johnson and John Cena don't *actually* hate each other. Sure, they put on a great show. But that shit's not real. Okay, so that I can sleep tonight, I'm just going to allow myself to believe that you knew that their whole wrestler rivalry is part of the act and I didn't ruin it for you.

Another great modern-era Benny and Allen bit, and what is probably my hands-down favorite, is happening now between two of my favorite people: Jimmy Kimmel and Matt Damon.

Supposedly it all started when at the end of his talk show Jimmy decided to turn to speak directly into the camera and sincerely apologize to Matt Damon for "running out of time" for his interview. Matt Damon was never supposed to be on that specific show, but the joke went over so well that Jimmy decided to continue to make similar comments over the next few years. Again, and again, he would sign off his show by apologizing to Matt for running out of time.

And after all of the apologies to Matt Damon for cutting his interview, Jimmy *finally* did have Matt on his show. And after a very lengthy introduction, a very defiant Matt walks out across the stage and sits down . . . and Jimmy turns to him and in a very straight face says,

Unfortunately, we are totally out of time.

Matt, of course, loses his shit, but in the best way. The network bleeps out what we are made to assume to be a diatribe of curses and expletives. It's a truly fantastic bit. But it doesn't stop there. What happens next is our modern-day Jack and Fred take things up a notch, and like, waaaay up.

They even go so far as to create *comedic sketches* around their newfound "feud." For example, Matt made a video with Jimmy's ex-girlfriend (Sarah Silverman) where they sing a song called "I'm Fucking Matt Damon." Then there's Jimmy's retaliation video with Ben Affleck called "I'm Fucking Ben Affleck." Then Jimmy has Guillermo (his sidekick on the show) in a sketch spoofing *The Bourne Identity* by having Guillermo play Matt's character of Jason Bourne. And just when you think it can't get any crazier, Jimmy comes out to do his monologue one night and says to the audience,

I don't want to bring you down, but there's some very sad news out of Hollywood this week . . . you probably heard: Matt Damon has a new movie coming out.

This could have been enough, but not for ol' Jimmy. He then proceeded to introduce the trailer of this "new film," which we find out is a prerecorded sketch made from footage of Matt Damon's film *The Martian*, but this trailer's narration sets up a very different, um, story. This movie is about a man looking for love and being all alone in outer space. The narration goes something like this . . .

. . . he did some deep exploration of his own. Because, sometimes, the greatest love of all is . . . under the zipper of your spacesuit.

Then the title:

Matt Damon is . . . The Mastronaut: Emission to Mars.

All of these sketches are super clever and fun. They all have a premise that is easy to follow. They all have a clever game, and they truly are heightened. In my humble opinion they are some of the greatest variety show sketches.

We asked Jimmy Kimmel if he was willing to comment on our musings about his and Matt Damon's Jack and Fred-esque "rivalry." And Jimmy's response was:

"I have read something about this in a story—about our ongoing 'feud'—but I didn't know about it until a couple of years ago.

I still don't know much about it."

Not unlike Milton Berle and Jack Benny, a comedic trailblazer named Sid Caesar also found ways to stretch the boundaries of variety on TV with *Your Show of Shows*. When it came to physical comedy, Sid was unmatched.

Joining him on his weekly show was a cast of regulars. And by "regulars," I'm referring to amazing talents, such as Imogene Coca and Carl Reiner, who both graced the stage for bits and sketches. By the way, Carl Reiner was also on the writing staff, along with a young writer named Mel Brooks . . . no big deal.

Sid Caesar created many incredible physical sketches using elaborate costumes and pantomime, a giant leap from the aural-only shows of his radio predecessors. Sid's performances were *visual* experiences, and ones that audiences couldn't get enough of.

For anyone who may not know, Mel Brooks is the creative genius behind some of the funniest and most influential comedy films of the twentieth century. We're talking *Blazing Saddles*; *History of the World, Part I*; *High Anxiety*; *Young Frankenstein*; and many more hilarious and classic comedies. He set bars, raised bars, and broke boundaries for what a comedy could be.

He was a frequent collaborator with the extraordinary comedic powerhouse that is Carl Reiner. They teamed up and created some pretty incredible sketches, including one of my favorites called the *2,000-Year-Old Man*. Carl also created and starred in many television shows and films until, sadly, he passed away in 2020. But even that very year he starred in the Quibi remake of *The Princess Bride*. The original version of the film was directed by his son Rob Reiner. A touching ending to an amazing career.

THE HISTORY OF SKETCH COMEDY

Mel Brooks

CHEAP APARTMENTS

A sketch is a little playlet. It's just a little play: a beginning, a middle, and an end. Very hard to get an ending where the premise would explode into a wonderful ending. Very hard. But we were pretty lucky on *Your Show of Shows*.

On *Your Show of Shows* (with Sid Caesar, and Imogene Coca, and the great Carl Reiner, and Howie Morris) we never did political humor, ever. We never made fun of the current president. We never rested our comedy on political stuff. It was always basically what was happening in society. It was societal. For instance, in the '50s, when the show was most popular, they built a lot of new apartment houses. They would spring up like chickens. It was just all over the place. There were a lot of apartment houses. And the apartment houses had thin walls, thin ceilings . . . they didn't put a lot into it. And one of our writers was living in a new apartment house and he said he couldn't sleep because the blue light from the neighbor's TV would invade his room through the walls. Sid said, "Why don't we do a sketch about these cheap apartment house's walls and ceilings?" So, we did. And Sid and Imogene were in the bedroom, and you saw the blue light go on, and you heard *The Jackie Gleason Show*. And then Sid says:

                              SID

      I'm gonna break the lease!

                           IMOGENE

      What are you gonna do?

                              SID

      Watch!

And he put on his robe, and he walked through ten apartments. Just
walked through the walls . . . smashed through the walls. He was a
strong guy. And people, you know, sitting up in bed in each one.

It was a wonderful sketch. And the reason for it was to draw attention
to what was, to what existed during our lives.

For example, there was a fantastic sketch called *The Bavarian Clock*. A narrator in voice-over sets up that there's a large, beautiful clock, like something you'd find in a town square. We learn that every day, the locals would watch the clock's mechanical figures come out with their hammers and chime the clock bell. When the hands of the clock reached 1:00 p.m., Sid, Carl, Imogene, and a performer named Howard Morris came out spinning and whirling in a very choreographed mechanical dance. They took turns hitting their hammers and ringing the clock chime.

This happens again and again with perfection . . . that is until the clock starts to break.

Once everyone caught on to this brilliant setup, audiences waited with bated breath to see how Sid and his cohorts would react, now that this perfect clock was malfunctioning. As this is one of the greatest comedic casts of all time, y'all knew that things were heading off the rails and someone was going to get water poured on their head. In this case it was Sid, and again, and again, and he played his (now wet) role with a straight face. His performance, and the entire bit, was in pantomime without any dialogue from Sid or his cast.

It was genius, and unlike anything anyone had ever seen before.

The Halcyon Days of Hayseed

In the early 1950s, Uncle Miltie, Sid Caesar, and the like reigned supreme. And, like most great reigns, this one also ran its royal course. It wasn't long before a new flavor of show was emerging, and that flavor was, well . . . let's say alfalfa, wheat, and barley. Allow me to explain: It seems the television networks had decided to set their hopes on capturing the rural audience, and the emergence of the country sitcom was the next big idea.

In 1957 a program called *The Real McCoys* came on the air. This show kicked off a movement toward programming that centered around the wholesome and naive characters that hailed from "the heartland." These were folks who had small-town adventures, and they didn't buy into that *gosh darn* allure of the big city.

So, as variety shows started to decline in the mid-'50s, here came the halcyon days of hayseed, with some hearty half-hour humors. These

Carol Burnett

SECOND BANANAS

My really *big* break was a hundred years ago with *The Garry Moore Show*. And he hired me as a second banana, and so I learned working with him. Garry was very generous. There was another second banana, Durward Kirby, on the show. I remember we would all sit around and be reading the script for that week. (Neil Simon was the junior writer on Garry's show.) So, we would be reading something and there might be a punch line or a joke at the end of a sketch, and Garry would look up and he'd say, "You know what, give this line to Carol" . . . or "give it to Durward." "They can say it funnier than I can." Which was so generous.

And that's the way I felt when I did my show. We had Harvey Korman and we had Vicki Lawrence, and Tim Conway and Lyle Waggoner; we were a true rep company. Yeah, my name was in the title, but there were sketches where Tim would be with Harvey, and Vicki would support Harvey, and Harvey would support me, and back and forth. We were a true rep company.

We rehearsed and rehearsed and rehearsed. The only time it kind of went crazy was when Conway went off script, which we loved. You know that didn't bother me. It didn't even bother the writers.

Where did the term *second banana* come from?

A comedian who supports another comedian who is the star of the scene or sketch is sometimes referred to as the second banana. It's not overtly clear where this concept originated. And even though it's a phrase I've heard of, I had to look this one up. Phil Silvers, a very popular comedian in the 1950s (who got his start in vaudeville as a kid), says that a comedian by the name of Harry Steppe coined the phrase in 1927. Its source is a routine that was chock-full of double talk, where three comics try to share two bananas. This makes sense to me. The first banana gets most of the laughs, and the other comic performer plays second fiddle to them. And . . . now I just need to find out where the term *second fiddle* comes from. I'm gonna go out on a limb and guess it's not from three people trying to share two fiddles.

were shows like *Petticoat Junction, The Andy Griffith Show, Mister Ed,* and *Lassie.* My two personal favorites of this era were *Green Acres* and *The Beverly Hillbillies*; one, because the reruns of these shows were some of the only shows on in the summer and two, because I lived in a neighborhood named Green Acres. Yes, I lived just south of 8 Mile Road in a neighborhood called *Green Acres.* Now let me explain something to you: Green Acres is (as you may have guessed) not the name of a neighborhood you would associate with Detroit. They really should have called it Gray Acres, because that shit was all concrete.

Both shows had rural themes that people could relate to. If you're not familiar, *Green Acres* was about a wealthy man who wants to give up the city life and move to a farm, and *The Beverly Hillbillies* was about a family that lived on a farm, struck oil, and then moved to Beverly Hills.

They are both different kinds of "fish out of water" stories about people who are out of place in their new world. This setup, of folks being out of their element, allows the writers to come up with limitless situations to create chaos and fun. In the comedic world we sometimes refer to these kinds of comedic opportunities as "joke buckets," as they are openings for the staff in a writers' room to fill up with bits.

The theme song for *The Beverly Hillbillies* is also really fun, and explains the story of their journey in a simple and catchy tune. It's one of those things that sticks with you. I'm humming it in my head right now. The song plays under the opening credits where we see the Clampett family when they first leave their farm and head to start their new life in Beverly Hills. And these mofos, they drive into town with all of their shit stacked up on top of one old rickety truck, looking like *Grapes of Wrath* up in here. It was crazy.

One of my favorite things on the show was that the Clampetts called their swimming pool "the ce-ment pond." That's my shit. The cement pond. Brilliant. Now *that* sounds like something one would find in Detroit.

With the exception of the variety show *Hee Haw*, most of these shows were situational comedies, a form that was on the upswing. By 1965, there were over thirty different sitcoms on the air. Now, that may not sound like a lot of shows, but we're talking about the era before cable, before streaming, when there were only three television channels. Three. Total. As in one, two, three. That's it. Three.

> *By 1965, there were over thirty different sitcoms on the air.*

Then, round about 1971, the networks and the powers that be made a complete about-face and wanted to get back to more urban fare. Why, you ask? Well, like everything else, it was about the almighty dollar. Attitudes and watching habits were evolving among the youth of our country and television was going along for the ride.

As the world was changing, and with the Vietnam War raging on overseas, younger audiences felt that the programming they were seeing on TV didn't reflect what was happening around them.

The one popular show that came closest to touching on the current events was a sitcom starring an actor and singer named Jim Nabors called *Gomer Pyle, U.S.M.C.* This show was straight up set on a military base in the present day (which back then was 1964 to 1969). My understanding is, and this fascinates me . . . that for the whole run of the show, they never actually mentioned the Vietnam War. Huh? Yup. Seems they wanted the

Jim Carrey

A LETTER FROM HOLLYWOOD

My history and lineage of sketch comedy begins as a child with *The Carol Burnett Show*. I was an insane fan of *The Carol Burnett Show*. I sent them a letter when I was ten years old trying to get myself on the show (because I did one hundred and fifteen impressions and I thought I could hang with Harvey Korman and Tim Conway).

I got a really sweet rejection letter back. And it was so exciting to me that I had gotten a letter from *Hollywood*, from Television City, and I went crazy with joy. Even though it was a rejection, it was a connection, to Carol Burnett.

Later on, I got to meet her. And, I got to do her anniversary special. I also got to meet Tim Conway. I was shocked at how incredibly sharp both of them were, and how quick-witted, and as artists how formidable they still were.

Carol Burnett. Smart as a fucking whip. When you meet her, when you talk to her for a little bit, and you joust with her a little bit, she'll come back, man. She's just sharp. You had to be sharp to live in that world, to not only exist, but to flourish in that world. You know how tough you had to be? Incredible. I have tons of respect. There were only a couple of women back then; her and Lucille Ball; just fucking survivors . . . like ninjas.

show to be entertaining, and be about the military, but never get political.

Showing our servicemen and -women under the light of a humorous situational comedy only worked for so long. Unfortunately, this kind of willful isolationism was keeping the younger, coveted, twenty-six- to thirty-five-year-old consumer from watching, and also in turn from buying car wax and refrigerators. The advertisers in the network saw this and decided to do something about it, and what they did became known as the "rural purge."

The big three networks started cutting back on all of the *rural*-themed shows and replacing them with ones that were more *urban* themed. So out goes *The Andy Griffith Show*; in comes the more metropolitan-themed *The Carol Burnett Show*. Also to go was a fantastic performer named Red Skelton, and in came Flip Wilson. Sadly, one of the casualties was also my beloved *Green Acres*. Pat Buttram, who played Mr. Haney on the show, was aptly quoted as saying,

> It was the year CBS canceled everything with a tree . . . including Lassie.

Yes, CBS joined the other networks and shifted their programming as well. But *Gomer Pyle* was extremely popular, and its star, Jim Nabors, was an asset. CBS didn't really want to lose this golden goose. So, after his show was canceled, they offered Jim, get this, his very own *variety* show. Yes indeedy.

Pet Rocks

As we moved into the 1970s, a whole new world of entertainers went out and joined this new variety circus, and television was never the same. For example, where can you find Peggy Fleming, Doug Henning, and Greg Evigan (from *B. J. and the Bear*) singing Christmas carols together? Now,

I'd like to say . . . nowhere, but in the 1970s and '80s, they were all guests on Donny and Marie Osmond's variety show. The Osmonds' impressive guest list also included current stars like Wolfman Jack, Milton Berle, Joey Travolta (yes, I said *Joey* Travolta), and even the Harlem Globetrotters.

As a child of the '70s and '80s, I truly feel blessed to have been part of a television culture that included singing acts, ice skating, magic shows, and massive amounts of canned laughter, called the American variety TV special. There's no joke too cheesy, no sketch too broad, or Donny Osmond sock too purple, for the good old U.S. of A., and we couldn't get enough of it . . . right down to every single Charo shimmy and oochie koochie. My girl talking 'bout oochie koochie. How's that your catchphrase, Charo? Your catchphrase is not even real words. Point being, it was an incredible time in entertainment.

Most of us are aware of the titans of the variety world, such as Sonny Bono, Cher, Flip Wilson, and Sid Caesar. There was also *The Smothers Brothers Comedy Hour, The Captain and Tennille*, and of course, everyone's beloved variety high bar, *The Carol Burnett Show*. But, did you know that *The Brady Bunch* also had a variety special? So did Dolly Parton, and Bette Midler, and even sports legend Howard Cosell.

It seemed like everyone in the 1970s had a variety show of their very own. It's as if they were handing them out like pet rocks. And, if you never had a pet rock, let me tell you it's not as exciting as it sounds. Okay, correction, it is *exactly* as exciting as it sounds. I did mention it was the '70s.

Sadly, not unlike the life span of a gag gift, some of these variety shows were also ultimately not meant to be. Mary Tyler Moore took a swing at variety, but her show didn't last very long. Now, to her credit, hers lasted longer than Sonny Bono's solo show called *The Sonny Comedy Revue*. Though Sonny had found success together with Cher, when they split, they both tried their hand with dueling projects. But alas, the world could only support about three weeks of a Cher-less Sonny.

> *It seemed like everyone in the 1970s had a variety show of their very own. It's as if they were handing them out like pet rocks.*

Perhaps, like me, you're wondering who decided that sequins would ever be a thing (not to mention confetti, ruffled tuxedo shirts, bell-bottoms, and feathered blowouts). I guess for our purposes, the more important question is how does all of this affect our subject at hand: sketch comedy.

Long gone were the days of Ed Sullivan with his novelty acts like plate spinning and chimps on a trapeze. These new shows were streamlined for the most part down to music and comedy acts. This format became a new breeding ground for sketch comedians, and a splashy updated variety show found its footing.

This new form of entertainment would go something like this: Sonny and Cher (for example) would open their show with a song, then launch into a little banter—a "duologue" if you will—then another song, then a comedic sketch with whoever was that week's guest. Most shows in the season would follow a similar menu. And other variety shows agreed that this was the way to go as well. Donny and Marie would usually start their show with dancers, sing a song, and then (like Sonny and Cher) do some cross talk, then a comic sketch, then perhaps another song or sketch with a guest star, such as the great Paul Lynde. This shuffling of acts continued until the end of the program, where they would finish with their signature song, "May Tomorrow Be a Perfect Day."

Even though television is a visual medium, and the colors and costumes and sets could be everything from elaborate to gaudy, to *very* elaborate and *very* gaudy, the influence of radio was still present. It's almost as if there were some growing pains, or at the very least the tried-and-true methods that worked for years in a nonvisual medium held up (and then some) on TV.

No matter how many visual elements performers had access to, the sketches that seemed to work the best, and get the biggest laughs, were often word- and banter-based. These could also be sketches that are filled with something known as "hard jokes." (These are jokes that have a clean punch line and would probably still be funny if you were to close your eyes and could only listen to them.) They aren't typically about physical characterization, and the emphasis doesn't need to be on set design, or some kind of super cool lighting. It's all about *how you tell a joke*.

If you aren't familiar with Paul Lynde, he's an actor and personality from the 1970s who was a guest star on shows like *The Patty Duke Show*, *The Flying Nun*, *Gidget*, and *The Munsters*. My favorite was when he was on *Hollywood Squares*. He'd usually be sitting in the coveted middle square and would always have the best one-liners. The host (Peter Marshall) would ask him survey questions like,

> *Does Ann Landers think there's anything wrong with you if you do your housework in the nude?*

And Paul Lynde would respond with something super pithy like,

> *No, but I have to be very careful when I'm doing my ironing.*

Or this one . . .

> HOST
>
> According to studies, will being breastfed make you smarter?
>
> PAUL
>
> Well, I missed three questions last week, so I'm willing to try anything.

Okay, last one. I promise.

> HOST
>
> According to the food editor of the *Dallas Morning News*, what's the best reason for pounding meat?
>
> PAUL
>
> Loneliness.

Let's just say the '70s were a special time.

For example, here's an exchange between Flip Wilson, star of *The Flip Wilson Show*, and his guest star, the incomparable Tim Conway. In this sketch, Flip and Tim stand behind an empty chair (which they are using as an all-purpose prop) and the scene starts with Tim looking down at the chair. He says,

That's a beautiful baby. Father of that baby is a handsome gentleman, I can tell that right now. Whose is it?

Then Flip steps up and responds,

I, sir, am the proud father.

                        TIM
    Oh really?

                        FLIP
    Yeah.

                        TIM
    Boy, he's a cute little guy.
    What's his name?

                              FLIP

          Elizabeth.

                              TIM

          Oh, I'm sorry . . . it's a girl.

                              FLIP

          No. It's a boy.

                              TIM

          Boy?

                              FLIP

          Yeah.

                              TIM

          Elizabeth?

                              FLIP

          Yeah.

                              TIM

          Okay. What do you call him? Liz?

                              FLIP

          No.
          We call him Junior.

    See what I mean? All the props and lighting and background actors in
the world wouldn't do anything to improve upon this. It's a perfect joke
that plays whether you're watching the scene or you hear it on the radio.

    And the same goes for the classic variety-host banter. For example,
take the opening of Sonny and Cher. All you need to know is that Sonny
is, let's say . . . *vertically challenged*, and you're off to the races. It's really
hard to miss the fact that he's short, as Cher reminds him, and us, over
and over again with her zingers. Cher would say something sincere like,

I don't know how to say this, but well . . . I told your mother to expect the patter of little feet around the house.

Then Sonny is completely taken aback and in awe says,

Oh, you're kidding, Cher. You mean, oh really? You mean . . . ?

And Cher would give him a very straight and dry,

I mean, yeah, that's right. You're sleeping at her house tonight.

You know what I'm saying? She just *Cher'd* the fuck out of him. She just went sha-swacks! You don't need any cameras. I'm Cher. That's my jam. Sorry buddy, you've been Cher'd. You can't see me right now, but I'm miming pushing my hair back and sticking my tongue out the side of my mouth. It's part of the whole gig. It's fun. You should try it if you haven't.

Sadly, on television today we don't see as many ice-skating acts, and we are no longer visited by Rip Taylor, who passed away. And if you came along after Rip Taylor, the king of confetti, look him up, and when you do, you'll say, "Wait, wait, this is what my parents thought was funny?" The answer is 100 percent yes. Rip Taylor had this thing where there'd be a punch line and then he'd do this crazy dramatic cackle laugh. You really can't do this today. If an actor, even a comedian, did something like that today they'd be picked up and taken to a sanatorium. What am I? A ninety-three-year-old from the South? A sanatorium? What I mean to say is, it was a bonkers thing for anyone to do.

My man once walked out onstage carrying a bra, and one of the cups was bigger than the other one. Then he'd wave it around and talk about,

Look, everybody. The Odd Couple! HELLOOOO!

Anyway, yes, yes, this was it. This was the height of my childhood comedy experience, a flamboyant gay man in sequins. The comedic version of being knighted was to be pelted with confetti by Rip Taylor. That was his bit. That was his deal. Another high point in '70s variety TV was getting to keep one of the aforementioned Donny Osmond purple socks, which Elle swears would be the greatest thing that could ever happen to any girl born before 1975. I'm sorry, the greatest thing? I'd like to remind her that she married me, but Donny Osmond? Fine. Okay. Elle's just no longer allowed to go to Utah. (The Osmonds live in Utah.) But seriously . . . Donny Osmond? I got my eye on you. He's like in his sixties. I can take him.

The comedic version of being knighted was to be pelted with confetti by Rip Taylor.

Now thankfully, as some variety shows started to get canceled, others were saved but relegated to late night spots. So, there is at least one stepchild of variety that's alive and well (for the most part) on TV and streaming this very day . . . *talk shows.*

Think about it. When you turn on Kimmel, Colbert, Cordon, or Fallon, what do you see? A host who does a monologue peppered with some jokes, then we come back from a commercial break and there could be a sketch with props, or there could be a game or some kind of musical parody. Then you may see a musical act, a stand-up comedian, and I don't know . . . a cooking or science demonstration. It hearkens back to the format of shows in the golden age. Pretty neat, right?

Now, I've been fortunate enough to be on Jimmy Fallon's *Late Night,* where I've played games, done musical impressions, and was also a guest star on a sketch called *Camp Winnipesaukee,* where I played a frustrated camp counselor to Jimmy and Justin Timberlake's misbehaving campers. The sketch was funny and short, but not as funny and short . . . as my shorts. Hell-o! Confetti! (That's for all you folks out there who enjoy a callback. And it's also for Rip Taylor, who made his own path and brought smiles to so many with his rubber chickens, gag underpants, and something called *The $1.98 Beauty Show.*)

Stephen Colbert
THE WORLD'S MOST HANDSOME HORSE

We recently had the world's most handsome horse on the show. I'm like, goddammit, I'm so excited, because this is a *real* variety show. There's no reason to have this horse on, other than to have a real horse onstage. He's really big, he's really handsome, and on the internet, people were getting off on the world's most handsome horse. He was like, shiny, kind of silvery, long mane. Kind of the . . . um . . . Fabio of draft horses.

He freaked out onstage and I would not go anywhere near him. He started to panic, and I thought I'm going to get trampled to death . . . and that would just be another act.

That would just be another act of the show . . . make sure to keep the cameras rolling as the EMS rolls in to cart off my crushed remains! As if that's just another variety act: people defibrillating me and removing the hoof from my neck.

Inspirational Celebrational Muppetational

As a child, before I was old enough to appreciate the finer humor of Dean Martin or Flip Wilson, my all-time favorite variety show was *The Muppet Show*. Yes, the Muppets were the hosts of some top-notch variety entertainment. They truly had everything from, well . . . puppets, to magic, to guest stars, all covered and then some. There was more cannonball catching, dancing monsters, and boomerang fish acts than anyone had ever seen. These motherfuckers even had pigs flying in space. Sorry. I mean *Piiiigs Iiiin Spaaaace*!

If that wasn't enough, there were also Muppet medical drama parodies, science-fiction parodies, and musical parodies. In fact, the members of the house band, The Electric Mayhem, were parodies themselves. The front man and piano player was Dr. Teeth, who was a cross between the New Orleans funkmeister Dr. John and the Pinball Wizard himself, Elton John. Rolf was a giant brown dog who sometimes sat in and played an old upright piano, and I believe was channeling the jazz legend Fats Waller. Janice, the namesake of Ms. Joplin, played tambourine and guitar and was intentionally designed with some Mick Jagger features, and ending up looking an awful lot like Carly Simon. Zoot was the saxophonist with his ever-present sunglasses, in a vibe that was so super cool it looked like he might  fall asleep, and was a throwback to a bunch of musicians. Then there was Floyd Pepper, whose name is an homage to Sergeant Pepper and Pink Floyd, but who bears a resemblance to Gregg Allman.

Finally, we get to my spirit "animal," who some say was straight up inspired by Keith Moon, the drummer from The Who. And somewhere in the late '70s, I would sit in front of the TV and at my homemade drum kit created by pots and pans balanced on books. Oh yes. I was poised and ready to wreak havoc on my copy of *The Cat in the Hat* and my mother's CorningWare with a wooden spoon. I did this because my favorite part of my favorite show was Animal. The Swedish Chef was my dad's, and he may

Animal, the drummer for the house band The Electric Mayhem, was my hero.

have had a thing for Miss Piggy too . . . but Animal, the drummer for the house band The Electric Mayhem, was my hero. His energy was infectious. He was brave and unbridled. And only recently have I come to understand just how much of an influence that crazy, unabashed, and unapologetic puppet, oh, excuse me . . . I mean, *Muppet*, would have on my life and my comedy.

Hey You Can't Do That

When variety shows were in their stride, there was no one more clever, charming, and creative than the stupendous Carol Burnett. Carol got her start on *The Garry Moore Show* and was given her own show in 1967, the groundbreaking and sublime *The Carol Burnett Show*.

A smart host knows how to surround herself with top-notch supporting players, and Harvey Korman, Tim Conway, and Vicki Lawrence were up to the challenge and then some.

This *Hey You Can't Do That* moment comes from the show's elaborate *Jaws* parody episode called "Jowls." Here, Harvey Korman and Tim Conway are in a sketch where they're playing fishermen who are sharing tragic stories from their time at sea.

In a very somber Robert Shaw–esque moment, Tim takes his turn to share his tale of tragedy. He takes his time, and his words are slow and deliberate.

                              TIM

          I lost a girlfriend . . . to the sharks.

                            HARVEY

          Oh, yeah?

And Tim, clearly distraught, continues,

                              TIM

          Yeah.

          Out in Hawaii.

          She was sitting on the front of a sailboat,

          jumped off and tried to swim to shore.

          Got about forty yards from shore . . .

          and then a big white hit her.

          She'd a made it too . . .

          if she hadn't been wearing

          her good luck ham.

What?! He said ham. Now you see, you can't do that! No, no, no, no, no. I'm straight up talking 'bout no!

You can't just say "good luck ham." My man said, "She all would've made it to the shore too, if she hadn't been wearing her good luck ham." No. You can't do that. Good luck ham. That is not a thing, nope, not a thing. Well, he did. But come on.

Talk about a good luck ham. What I want to know is, how do you wear one anyway?? Like was it on a necklace? Did she have it on a chain? I mean, really . . . if you gonna wear anything, maybe don't use a whole ham. I guess you can make a pendant or something, but just like with a piece of bacon.

CHAPTER 6

The British Are Coming, the British Are Coming!

The British are coming. The British are coming. Thank you, Paul Revere. Both Paul Reveres, actually: Paul Revere the patriot and Paul Revere, the guy who's the lead singer of the band Paul Revere and the Raiders, who were a very committed band.

I'm just going to go on this tangent for a moment. Paul Revere and the Raiders were a 1960s American rock band who wore colonial garb while they were singing rock and roll songs. That's commitment. It takes a lot of guts to be like, "I'm just going to get onstage wearing tails, high boots, a petticoat, and a waistcoat" (or a *weskit*, as the Brits would say). I don't know if the band always performed that way, but it was on one of their album covers, and in some of their videos, so I would like to believe that's how they did all of their shows.

But thankfully, this chapter is about actual Brits, the talented comedic trailblazers that hail from the other side of the world, on that cluster of islands off the coast of mainland Europe.

To start simply, the Brits are a very polite people . . . at least the ones that I have come in contact with in my life. And it's not surprising that a lot of their comedy is very subtle and sophisticated. Part of that comes from the culture of politeness, which they have embraced.

As an American, I am in awe of this phenomenon. It fascinates me. If I'm in London and get into a black cab on Oxford Street, the decency that comes across from the cab driver really stands out. All I have to do is give the driver an address and what I would get in return, with a smile, would be . . .

Oh, good morning to you. Oh, you're heading to Marble Arch, are you? Well, you're up for a fancy afternoon. And we've got some good weather for you too. Never sunny like this. Usually raining. Don't know if you've heard that, right? "Foggy London" and all that.

Yes. I have heard that. I have heard that, actually.

Oh, you have? Oh, good for you. All right. A well-traveled man.

Now he's complimenting me? Seriously. A cab driver. Unheard of. At least it's very different than what anyone is used to getting if they live in New York, like I do.

Ah yes, decency. The Brits are decent. They're polite. And lots of their work is filled with this kind of clever, polite charm. That is, until it isn't. What I mean by that is they can do this wonderful thing where they do comedy that *sounds* polite and can also be deliciously wicked at the same time. They are a clever bunch for sure.

If you didn't know, in England, sketch comedy is considered a high art form and it is celebrated as such. And rightly so, as these men and women are courageous trailblazers who have influenced comedy around the world.

Somewhere near the turn of the century, amateur comedy troupes started forming at universities in the United Kingdom. And to clarify, for anyone under the age of twenty, when an older gentlemen (like myself) says, "turn of the century," you can assume we mean going from the 1800s to the 1900s, and not the more recent time period when *X-Men* was hitting the movie theaters, and Justin Bieber was in kindergarten.

Speaking of higher learning . . . there is a university in Cambridge, aptly called Cambridge University. And in 1883, a group of students

If you've ever had the pleasure of being in a New York City cab, you may have experienced a different kind of driver. Instead of lovely chats about the weather or the dishing of compliments, perhaps you've gotten some form of this . . .

No way, I ain't going to Harlem. My shift's almost over. You want me to get stuck in tunnel traffic? What, are you fucking nuts?

And by the way, if a New York City cab driver (or if anyone in New York City, or *from* New York City) ever says to you, *You want me to get stuck in tunnel traffic?* Or, *What, are you fucking nuts?*, please do not respond. If you live anywhere else in the world, these phrases will most likely *sound* like a question and probably are. But trust me on this, in New York City, they are not questions. "What are you, fucking nuts?" is 100 percent a statement. I guess it could be a question and a statement put together. Maybe it's even a kind of a hypothetical *quate-ment*. But the bottom line is, it's not something you should ever answer. In the wise words of G.I. Joe, *Now you know, and knowing is half the battle.*

started the Cambridge University Footlights Dramatic Club (or Cambridge Footlights, for short). Every year, they would put on a type of show called a "revue." And in this show, they would sing songs and perform comedy sketches and witty monologues. There was also a troupe called the Oxford Revue. In many ways both of these places are similar to The Second City in the States, where Mike Myers, and Dan Aykroyd, and Tina Fey, and I honed our skills.

The Oxford Revue and the Cambridge Footlights were breeding grounds for a handful of extremely talented performers. Perhaps you're familiar with some of them: John Cleese, Michael Palin, Peter Cook, Dudley Moore, and Rowan Atkinson (aka Mr. Bean). These folks are Herculean heroes in the sketch comedy world.

Something that is very special and specific to the Brits and sketch is their use of wordplay. Sure, there's a lot of physical comedy in British

Comedy is so beloved in the United Kingdom that to many it's even, dare I say, a noble profession. Some folks have even been given knighthoods. I know we don't have knighthoods in the US but it would be pretty cool if we did: Sir Eddie Murphy? Sir Jordan Peele? That works for me. Sir Carrot Top? Sure, why not.

sketch, but it's how they deal with language that I think elevates their work. Both Peter Cook and Dudley Moore were masters at wordplay. And when they joined forces, everyone had a good evening, which happens to be the name of one of their most popular comedy revues. In their show *Good Evening* they performed sketch after brilliant sketch sharing their outlandish, but somehow still relatable perspectives of situations and events. And they did this with so much ease and aplomb; in the 1960s they were *the ones to watch*.

> *Something that is very special and specific to the Brits and sketch is their use of wordplay.*

They held a steady place at the forefront of English satire.

Cook and Moore met in a sketch comedy troupe called Beyond the Fringe. Two members of their group were from the Oxford Revue, and two members were from the Cambridge Footlights, and they all came together and they made this supergroup. It's like if you put Jon Bon Jovi in a band, with, well . . . I dunno, just pretty much stick Bon Jovi with like about anybody else and you got yourself a supergroup. That was this.

There are two sketches in particular from their revue *Good Evening* that I think are just stellar. One of them is called *The Frog and Peach*. This sketch begins when the lights come up on two men onstage during a TV interview. And it goes something like this:

DUDLEY

Good evening. I'm talking tonight to Sir Arthur Greeb-Streebling.

Christopher Guest

BEYOND THE FRINGE

My first connection in comedy was with the four gentlemen of Beyond the Fringe in the late '50s. And I got to know Jonathan Miller very well and work with him. And I got to work with Peter Cook as well. They were really the first, of anyone, to be extremely smart and funny and do this groundbreaking show which I saw in London when I was twelve. And that was the precursor of what became John Cleese's group [Monty Python]. But they were really the first people to not just do sort of "knock down" stuff. This was an extremely smart group of people from either Oxford or Cambridge; and they were all highly intelligent and funny, which was kind of novel. That's just who they were. I mean, Jonathan Miller was a neurologist and the other guys were writers, and Dudley was a musician, and Allan Bennett was a great playwright, and there was this kind of rarified air. And so, for me it very was eye-opening to be a young kid, to see that and then to think: wow that's a pretty high bar. I had seen movies, ostensibly funny movies, but this really kinda shook my head a bit, and it had an effect on what I did later.

                         PETER

No, you're not.

                         DUDLEY

I'm not?

                         PETER

You're not at all. No. You're talking to Sir Arthur
Streeb-Greebling.

                         DUDLEY

Oh, oh, oh. Yeah.

                         PETER

No. You're confusing me with Sir Arthur Greeb-
Streebling.

                         DUDLEY

Oh. Yes. I'm so sorry.

                         PETER

Yes. My name is Sir Arthur Streeb-Greebling. The T is
silent, as in fox.

                        [Beat]

Yes, that's what the dude said. *T* is silent as in fox? Brother, please.
Mind blown.

Anyhow, Dudley continues to ask Peter Cook about his new restaurant,
called The Frog and Peach, and the inspiration behind it. Peter responds
to him with,

                         PETER

Where could a young couple go with not too much money
to spend, feeling a bit hungry, feeling a bit peckish,
want something to eat? Where can they go and get a
really big frog? A really big frog and a damn fine
peach? Where can they go? Where can they go? Yes. Yes.

```
Where can they go? Of course, the answer came there,
none. So, on this premise, I founded this restaurant.

                        DUDLEY

And how long ago did you start this venture?

                        PETER

Oh, that's a tricky one. Let's see. Certainly within
living memory.
```

Within living memory. That's my jam.

```
                     PETER (CONT.)

I believe it was shortly after World War II. You
remember that, World War II? Absolutely ghastly
business. Yes.

I was completely against it.

                        DUDLEY

Well, I think we all were.

                        PETER

Yes. Well, I wrote a letter.
```

My man wrote a letter. Now, see, that's fantastic. You can't just say you wrote a letter. I mean, who's he writing? Who you going to address that to . . . to the world . . . ? Hmm. I am really upset about this world war thing, let me see, "Dear . . . um . . . the whole wide world."

And yes, this got me. Cook and Moore got me. Their skewed perception, their deft verbal games, and the way that they were able to express themselves was absolutely groundbreaking. And can you see what I mean about the wordplay? Playing with language, and again, all that civility and politeness they keep throwing in that mix. Love this. By the way, the *T* is silent as in fox—my hands-down favorite line of the sketch.

The T *is silent as in fox.*

There is another piece that not only does a brilliant job at highlighting that politeness theme, but also is arguably the most popular

Bob Odenkirk

THIS BLOKE CAME UP TO ME

To point to one thing that I hope people look up . . . it would be Peter Cook and Dudley Moore, and the bit *This Bloke Came Up to Me*. So, it's Derek and Clive, and it's the greatest example of the most organic, natural, surprising improv sketch heightening that there is. It starts with Dudley Moore doing his character, talking about this guy coming up to him in a bar and saying something mildly insulting and causing an argument. And then the most interesting thing about it is Peter Cook builds on Dudley Moore's premise by telling his own story about a bloke who came up to *him* and said,

Hey.

And I said,

Don't you say HEY to me.

And he builds on it with no build. And it's just beautiful. Because it's funnier than what Dudley Moore said, and it's *less* of a premise, by a lot. It's *no* premise. The premise is that the guy is being insulted—just because the person came up to him. And it's beautiful. It's a beautiful example of "yes-anding" that actually diminishes, in a way, the initial premise and by doing so builds out the emotional impact of the exchange. It's just something to hear and marvel at.

A lot of times, improvisers (especially) get caught in a cleverness loop where whatever the premise is, the actors get a hold of a twist on that premise and they just try to *outdo* each other by building it bigger and bigger. And that certainly can be funny, and you can have a laugh reaction to that. But for this improv sketch (and I still don't know whether they improvised the whole thing) Peter Cook builds this sketch by kind of *dropping backwards* and letting the emotion of the sketch be more important than the concept. It's worth looking at. I love it so much. It's one of my favorite things.

sketch of the show and one of my all-time favorites. The sketch is called *One Leg Too Few*.

This sketch starts with Peter alone onstage calling out for someone to send in the next applicant. Dudley then enters for what we soon learn is an audition for an acting role. Dudley is wearing a raincoat, but like a giant raincoat. This coat expertly hides the leg that Dudley has bent behind him, as the character he's portraying is that of a man with only one leg.

Somehow, he managed to fasten his bent leg back so Dudley can have both of his hands free. My man enters hopping, and he's just hopping up and down on his one free leg *for the length of the scene*. Yes, all true; during the entire scene he's bopping around the stage on one freakin' leg. It's truly a spectacle to watch. And my man doesn't have crutches or a cane. That's some straight-up commitment to his art right there.

Extra layers like this add to our enjoyment of the sketch. It allows the audience to enjoy a sketch on two or three or more levels. And it's great when something's funny and you think you have it figured out and then there's a twist. And *then* there's another twist on the twist. And that always makes for good sketch. Adding to a scene is called *heightening*. And this particular scene is mountainous.

> It's great when something's funny and you think you have it figured out and then there's a twist.

This scene is also a great example of that thing in sketch comedy we refer to as "game." When you see a really great sketch, one that sticks with you, one that has you shaking your head at the screen or, even better, one that makes you want to yell at the actors on the screen 'cause they got you good—chances are pretty high that the reason you loved that sketch is because it had some kind *of game*. In most great sketches there is usually a game. And if you're lucky, there could even be more games stacked on top of the first game. Some games can be super easy and straightforward, while other games can even get somewhat meta.

In *One Leg Too Few* there is the joke (or the game) of the scene, which I'm going to share with you in a second, and then another game on top of

In most great sketches there is usually a game.

that one that's super fun, which is that you have no idea how long he's going to be able to hop. And you can't watch the sketch without waiting for him to lose his balance. I mean he can't possibly keep this up for the whole sketch? Or . . . can he?

So anyway, back to this scene . . . Dudley's hopping around, he's hopping around, he's hopping, pretty much underneath the entire scene. Dudley crosses the stage and is greeted by Peter Cook:

                    PETER

        Oh, Mr. Spigot, I believe.

                    DUDLEY

        Yes. Spigot's my name.

                    PETER

        Now, you're auditioning for the role of . . .
        Tarzan?

                    DUDLEY

        Yes. Yes.

                    PETER

        Oh, I couldn't help noticing almost immediately, Mr.
        Spigot, that you are a one-legged man.

                    DUDLEY

        Oh, well you noticed.

                    PETER

        Yes. Yeah. When you've been in the trade as long as I
        have, you do notice these things almost instinctively.

                              DUDLEY

Oh, I see.

                              PETER

But you are auditioning for the role of Tarzan.

                              DUDLEY

That is so.

                              PETER

A role which traditionally involves a two-legged
artiste.

                              DUDLEY

Definitely.

                              PETER

But you . . . a one-legged man . . . a uni-dexter, are
applying for the role?

   Uni-dexter. Favorite line. One of my favorite words in all of sketch
comedy.

                              DUDLEY

Yes, yes.

                              PETER

A role for which two legs would seem to be the minimum
requirement.

                              DUDLEY

Yes.

                              PETER

Well, Mr. Spigot, need I point out to you where your
deficiency lies with regard to your landing this
vital role.

Well, I think you ought to.

PETER

Need I say with over much emphasis that it is in
the . . . leg division you are deficient. Yes. It is
in the leg division, you are deficient.

DUDLEY

Ah. Oh, I see. Right. Yes. The leg division.

PETER

Yes. Your right leg I like. Very much. Yes. It's an
ideal leg for the role. Well, I have nothing against
your right leg.

[Beat]

The trouble is . . . neither have you.

Fan . . . tas . . . tic. And, you see what I mean about coming at things from a different perspective and pushing boundaries, right? Not to mention this civility. This is a perfect example of having a game and heightening. There is hope, however. The interviewer continues,

PETER

Well, don't despair, Mr. Spigot, you'll score over a
man with no legs. You'll have a definite advantage
over a man with no legs at all. In fact, if a legless
man was to come in here, I'd have no hesitation in
saying to him, "Get out, run away." So, there is still
a chance. There's a very, very good chance. If we do
not get any two-legged actors in here in the next two
weeks, you are exactly the sort of chap we should be
trying to contact.

Besides the provocative awkwardness of the situation, some of the biggest laughs in the scene come from watching Dudley Moore trying to stay upright. Which, although he does his job masterfully, every time I watch it, I'm STILL waiting for him to lose his balance or I don't know, pass out, or both. And the beauty of it is that he knows this. He knows he's playing this extra *game* and he uses it against us, and against poor Peter, by trying to make Peter break or laugh.

At one point Dudley hops over to a desk that's on the stage and then he leans his arm onto the desk and he stops hopping for a moment to catch his breath. And you know this motherfucker's exhausted, but he leans on the desk, I mean really leans, and uber dramatically pretends that he's very interested in what Peter is saying, but really what he's doing is trying to get Peter to break while he's giving his own leg, well, a break.

Four Candles

Another popular team of wordplay pros was *The Two Ronnies*. *The Two Ronnies* was a BBC sketch show, starring Ronnie Corbett and Ronnie Barker. And they were fantastic. I would say a lion's share of their sketches consisted of wordplay. They had some pretty extraordinary sketches around mispronouncing a word to mean something different than you were thinking, as the word may have multiple meanings. When a word can be used one way, but it can also mean something totally different and maybe not

"Breaking" in a sketch is what happens when a performer finds something so funny that, try as they might, they have a reaction and can't stay in character. Someone may in turn smile or laugh out loud, even though it's not part of the acting choices they've made and doesn't fit within the confines of the scene. Or better yet, when something surprises an actor or catches them off guard and then they try with all of their might to *not* laugh, and the audience sees the actor making those *trying really hard not to laugh faces*, which I think is even more funny. The bottom line is, no matter how someone goes off script when something is funny, if they are breaking character, they are "breaking."

entirely appropriate, it is known as a *double entendre* (which sounds very French because it is).

And one of my top ten all-time British wordplay sketches comes from their show. The setup is super simple. It's just a man who walks into a store with a list of items that he's looking to purchase. And yeah, that's pretty much it. The guy enters and walks up to the gentleman behind the counter and asks for,

For-kandles.

And, by the way, both guys are super cockney, and that's a very important key to the scene. And with a confident tone the salesman replies,

Four candles. Okay. Four candles . . .

The shopkeeper goes to look for them, and then he returns and he puts the candles on the counter and the customer says,

No. For-kandles.

> SALESMAN
>
> Here you are. Four candles.
>
> CUSTOMER
>
> No, no, no. For-kandles. Fork-'andles. Handles for forks.
>
> SALESMAN
>
> Oh. Oh no, no, no, no. We haven't gotten any, we haven't gotten any.
>
> CUSTOMER
>
> Oh, all right.
>
> CUSTOMER
>
> Got any 'ohs?

> SALESMAN

'Ohs?

> CUSTOMER

'Ohs.

So, then the shopkeeper grabs a garden hoe, and he brings it back to the guy and the guy's looking at him and the guy's like,

> CUSTOMER

No, no, no, 'ohs. I need 'ohs.

> SALESMAN

Oh, 'ohs. Right. I thought you meant 'ohs.

> CUSTOMER

No, no, no, no. I meant 'ohs. I meant 'ohs.

> SALESMAN

You meant 'ohs then you should have said that, all right. 'Ohs.

He said, *'ohs*, he meant *'ohs*. And he walks off to go find the thing.

So, he's rummaging around. And then he grabs a garden hose, brings it back to the counter, and sets it down.

All right. There you are. 'Ose.

> CUSTOMER

No, no. 'Ohs!!

> SALESMAN

Oh, you mean panty-ose?

> CUSTOMER

No, I mean 'ohs, 'ohs!!

SALESMAN

You're having me on . . . ?

It's hilarious. These motherfuckers up here talking about, 'ohs. 'o's. 'oze . . . Ain't nobody kings of wordplay like *The Two Ronnies*. And by the way, the line "You're having me on" means "Are you mocking me?" And thankfully *The Two Ronnies* were mocking all of us. The premise of a scene like this is something really, really, really fun. And when I use the word *premise*, I do also mean the game; the game of the scene is super fun.

This comedic game is usually a pattern where once the audience catches up to, or figures out the pattern of the game, they can play along. The game in this scene is that for every item our frustrated customer wants to purchase, there are multiple items in the store that sound like whatever the words are coming out of his mouth. That's the game. And more often than not this type of setup is what makes a sketch funny. And usually, it gets even funnier the more you understand the pattern, and the more you are in on the joke.

We humans love patterns. So, finding the pattern in the scene makes us happy. I find this very interesting because what makes us laugh, more often than not, is *uncomfortability*. I can explain. What happens in this kind of sketch is pattern, pattern, pattern, pattern, then the actors break the pattern in a way that you're not expecting, and that makes us laugh.

In this particular sketch we try to get ahead of the pattern. We hear the name of the item, and our brains start having a field day, trying to guess what the item is that the shopkeeper will bring over that is the wrong thing, while also trying to guess what the customer actually wants. And this specific sketch is fairly easy to track down if you want to know the answer as to what 'ohs my man was actually referring to. *The Two Ronnies: Fork Handles*. Okay, maybe that's just a sneaky way for me to get you to enjoy a journey down a Ronnie and Ronnie rabbit 'ole.

Gary Oldman

A RICHARD THE THIRD

For me it was Tony Hancock, The Goons, Peter Cook, Dudley Moore, Monty Python, and *The Two Ronnies.* Gotta' have *The Two Ronnies.* Ronnie Barker and Ronnie Corbett. Grew up on that. And of course, the writing, the writing was absolutely top rate. Like all the great comedians and all the great comics, it's observation, and then it's ever so slightly heightened. You're familiar with it. There's a tone or an atmosphere you're comfortable with and then you're willing to go with them.

The sketches, many of them, they're genius. Ronnie Barker does a sketch where he is a priest giving a sort of eulogy, or it's like a sermon or something. It's just him, like on a pulpit, and he does his thing. But, he does it all in cockney rhyming slang. So, he tells the story about *"a Richard the Third"* and how people don't want to pick it up or tread on it. And of course, the way the story sounds is that it's a *Richard the Third*—a *turd*. He leads you to believe that it's a shit on the sidewalk, but actually it's a *Dickie bird*. He does the entire sermon in cockney rhyming slang. And it's just genius. Wonderful stuff.

Garvey's Got Game

One of the most popular sketches on *Key & Peele* has a really phenomenal word game in it. The sketch I'm referring to is called *The Substitute Teacher*. I play a character named Mr. Garvey, who is an inner-city teacher who gets called to sub at an upper-middle-class school somewhere in the suburbs.

So, what happens is because of where he's from (and the experience of inner-city kids he's accustomed to dealing with) he makes certain assumptions about what to expect from this new group of very white, and very well-behaved, teens. The audience very quickly learns how off base he is. He begins by reading names off the roll sheet to take attendance. And because of who he is and the environment he's used to, he makes some pretty specific choices about how the kids' names should be pronounced.

The game here is trying to guess what name the substitute teacher is going to call out, and then also to guess what the student's name *actually is*. And as an added bonus, watching the frustration of everyone involved is pretty fun as well.

For example, Mr. Garvey starts by calling out for a student named . . .

Jay-quelin.

So, when we (the audience) hear "Jay-quelin," we join up with the students in the room who aren't sure who he's referring to. Everyone together is like, What's a Jay-quelin? Who's a Jay-quelin?

And then one girl finally bravely raises her hand and with some trepidation says,

Do you mean . . . Jacqueline?

Boom. The game starts . . . or more like *the game is afoot* (since we're on a chapter about the Brits). So, now we all understand a little bit about what's going to be happening for the next three

minutes of your life. And maybe you're not going to be able to beat Mr. Garvey to the punch, but part of the fun is trying to. The scene continues with Mr. Garvey looking for other students, including one named *D-Nice*, then an *A-A-Ron*, and even a *Bal-lockay*.

This game, and the sketch around it, has become so popular that sometimes I can't walk down a crowded street without someone yelling out,

Hey, A-A-Ron!

Or another common one . . .

Hey, yo, my name's Blake and everybody at work calls me Bal-lockay.

Or someone says,

My name's Rebecca. Can you say it funny for me?

And I'm just like,

That's just too easy. Rebbe-Kay. Where are you at, Rebbe-kay? I got my eye on you, Rebbe-kay.

And then that Rebecca woman loses her damn mind.

This kind of language game goes all the way back to the British comedic writer known as *Willy-ham Shake-a-spearay*. In the fifteenth and sixteenth centuries they didn't have cell phones, they didn't have Fortnite, they didn't even have Atari Pong. Instead, they filled their entertainment with stages and wordplay, and it was a super popular game that was thoroughly enjoyed.

Are We the Naughties?

When it comes to British humor, it's all good, clean fun . . . except for when it's super filthy, dirty, and that *double entendre* fun. Now, what do I mean by that? It's kind of this weird line because sometimes there is a world where those Brits fly their scandalous flag. But it's never that they're disgusting . . . it's more that they're kinda naughty, maybe.

Matt Lucas

FRIENDS ARE COOL

As far as an aspect of something that differs in British comedy programs versus those in America; I think that we often look at American comedies as more aspirational than British comedies. The people in American shows are more "cool," and better looking ... and more successful. If you look at an American sitcom, it takes place in the apartment where you want to live, like in the show *Friends.* And, by the way, all of those people on *Friends* also look great. In British comedy the characters for the most part live in places where you wouldn't want to be. Look at *Mr. Bean,* and Victor Meldrew from *One Foot in the Grave,* and David Brent, and Basil Fawlty from *Fawlty Towers* ... British comedy is usually about failure.

The Brits can even be classy and disgusting at the same time. It's not just that somebody's farting. It's that Henry V, king of England, is farting. Or that it's Ulysses from Shakespeare's *Troilus and Cressida* is farting. And it's like, *Oh, well, excuse you, Joan of Arc.* See? Classy. And in shows like *Little Britain*, *The Benny Hill Show*, and even *Absolutely Fabulous*, there are scenarios and sketches where a lot of inappropriate behavior ensues. But even though they're inappropriate, it somehow still seems polite.

Now, Benny Hill. How can I describe Benny Hill? Let's just put it this way. He was one of the greatest practitioners of lowest common denominator comedy. And, what I mean by that is his sketches trafficked in things like boozing, arguing with his wife, and well, lots of boob-ogling. That's really what he did. Lots of boobs. And the folks across the pond, they loved him. And they loved him here in the States as well.

I was maybe thirteen when I first saw a *Benny Hill* sketch, and I was 100 percent too young to have seen a *Benny Hill* sketch. For example, I still remember to this day a scene where Benny's character sits on the front porch and calls over a local young woman. She's very busty and has a very low neckline, and Benny is of course staring at her chest when he says,

My god, you've grown out . . . up.

Then he continues . . .

I reckon you can take a shower without getting your feet wet.

YOUNG WOMAN
I bet you could too.

He makes a comment that he's impressed with her comeback.

YOUNG WOMAN
Well, I usually give tit for tat.

BENNY
Well, in that case . . . tat.

Yessir-y. That pretty much sums up a large portion of the jokes that took place on *Benny Hill*. Different days, different girls, but usually similar tats. Even though he was "edgy" at the time, I think it's understandable why we don't see too much of Benny Hill these days.

Absolutely Fabulous isn't a sketch show per se, but Jennifer Saunders and Joanna Lumley, the show's leads, have done a masterful job creating scenarios with such brilliant setups that can truly stand on their own as sketches. And a lot of them were inappropriate and brash . . . from escapades in a hospital room (including complaining that there's no minibar), to getting stuck on a luggage carousel in the airport; they have found incredible ways to bring a premise, an escalation, and a button to a whole 'nother level.

There's a great example of character building through physicality in the show *Little Britain*. There are two characters named Lou and Andy who are played by the uber-talented actors David Walliams and Matt Lucas. Lou is a caregiver to Andy, as Andy is "wheelchair bound." I put those words in quotes for a reason. In one of the funniest sketches I've ever seen in my life, Lou wheels Andy to a swimming pool, and goes to ask a gentleman if he would be willing to help him get his friend, his invalid friend, in and out of the pool as it's a challenge to do so. A *kerfuffle*, I believe is the word he uses.

Now, as he's describing the process to this gentleman and asking him for his assistance, in the background we see Andy who has clearly has gotten out of his chair, and is running (with his perfectly working legs) full speed to the area with the diving boards. He climbs up the three flights to the top of the highest diving board, dives off the board and into the pool, then swims to the side, gets out of the pool, and goes back to his wheelchair. He sits down just in time for Lou to turn around. And then of course he's wet and Lou doesn't have any idea why.

It's a very simple, straightforward game of someone pretending to be something he isn't, and the physical choices Matt Lucas makes for his character's actions do a lot to speak to who he is and his personality. And it's also funny as shit.

The other thing the Brits do that sets them apart is a lot of historical humor. I guess if your country's been around pretty much as long as the Romans, then you're going to have quite a lot of history to pull from. They'll write sketches about Shakespeare. They'll write sketches about kings and queens, about Druids. Whereas, in the United States, a lot of our sketch is about *current* events. On *SNL*, *In Living Color*, and other shows, you'll occasionally find historical subject matter in sketches, and even some scenes in period costume. But, in British comedy, it's done much more frequently, and certainly with some old-school aplomb. I've seen the Brits do sketches about the Magna Carta, Guy Fawkes, there's even a sketch about the Treaty of Westphalia, whatever the heck that is.

There was a fairly recent show in England called *That Mitchell and Webb Look*. I *love* a sketch of theirs where there are two men playing Nazis on the front line of the Russian frontier. And the scene goes something like this:

                    SOLDIER 1

    They're coming. Now, we'll see how these Russians deal
    with a crack SS division.

                    SOLDIER 2

    Hans.

                    SOLDIER 1

    Have courage, my friend.

                    SOLDIER 2

    Yeah. Hans. I've just noticed something.

                    SOLDIER 1

    Yeah, these communists are all cowards.

                    SOLDIER 2

    Have you looked at our caps recently?

                    SOLDIER 1

    Our caps?

                    SOLDIER 2

    The badges on our caps. Have you looked at them?

```
                    SOLDIER 1

What? No. A bit.

                    SOLDIER 2

They've got skulls on them.

Have you noticed that our caps have actually little
skulls on them?

                    SOLDIER 1

I don't think so.

                    SOLDIER 2

Hans.

Are we . . .

the baddies?
```

I love my man *just* realized that something is off. The dudes got skulls on their hats. Seems like a telling sign to me. Hey, are you a good guy or a bad guy? Not sure? Do you have a rainbow or maybe a turtledove on your hat? No? Hang on, brother, do you have a black uniform with skulls on it? You do? Well, maybe you should consider taking that hat off and find another line of work. Just saying.

The Ministry of Silly Everything

If I, or just about anyone working in sketch today, were to pick one British comedy team who had the most influence on American sketch comedy, it would have to be John Cleese, Terry Gilliam, Eric Idle, Michael Palin, Graham Chapman, and Terry Jones. They are Monty Python. They are the reigning gold medalists in pretty much every comedic sport. They are the crème de la crème. Their absurdity is unmatched. They threw away rules and turned every convention on its head.

But before we get too far along on a Python path, I would like to share some work from one of *their* influences. You may remember when we mentioned something called British music hall. In British music hall the

John Oliver

ACUTELY OBSERVED

The thing that was really significant to me (other than *Monty Python* and *Fry and Laurie*) was *The Day Today*, which spouted Steve Coogan and Chris Morris. It came out of this radio show they did called *On the Hour*, which was basically a sketch show within the construct of a news program. And it was so far ahead of its time in terms of what news became. Because all they did was, kinda take news and turn it up 20 percent. They did 120 percent proof of the news, making it truly ridiculous, but still within the world of what it currently was.

What I loved about *The Day Today* and *On the Hour* is it was so polished. It was like a jus sauce production; everything was reduced and reduced and reduced until they are perfect sketches. Word. Perfect. And it seems like we're going through a phase where (and not that this is a bad thing) but where sketches online and especially on TikTok, and YouTube, are a little more rough and ready. That's their charm. What I loved about *The Day Today* back then was that you could feel the obsession. "We have twenty-nine minutes to get this right. So, I'm going to make this as dense as I can and make every single joke in this as good as I possibly can." It was your classic six episodes, your British six episodes, and kind of word perfect.

sketches usually follow, what we consider, a very traditional format. There was usually a premise, with some kind of an escalation, and then a button.

Out of that world came *The Goon Show*. Members of the group included Harry Secombe, Spike Milligan, and a man named Michael Bentine (who left the show early in its run). Another member was Peter Sellers. (Some people know Peter Sellers best from when he played the Pink Panther in *The Pink Panther* movies in the 1970s.)

So, these guys put together a radio show in front of a live audience. They created a bunch of recurring characters that would travel all over the world and have wacky adventures. They just smashed all the rules of everything, even of the time-space continuum. They would do these amazing things where sometimes one guy would leave the room and then he'd come back in the room as if he was in a time warp or a loop. And this is the 1950s that they were doing stuff like this. And whatever they were doing, their audiences would be howling with laughter.

> *There was usually a premise, with some kind of an escalation, and then a button.*

There was one little sketch that they did where they were out in the woods and Harry Secombe's character says,

Over there, go, go, go knock on that oyster.

Yes, that's right, this dude says, "Go knock on that oyster." They don't even pretend to justify why someone would live in an oyster.

Over there, knock on the oyster.

So one of the other guys goes over to it and he "knocks" on the oyster. And then from the inside of the oyster we hear the patter of feet coming down what seems to be a very long hallway. Patter, patter, patter, patter, patter . . . and on and on. Then they *finally* get to the door and you hear a voice say,

Yes . . . ?

The dude just walked sixteen million feet inside of an oyster. And he goes, "Yes?" Like no big deal. I guess that's how insides of oysters just are. And then my man outside says,

Is Pearl in?

No. What. Is Pearl in? Please. And then the voice says,

Oh, no. Pearl's not in, but I'm her mother . . .

And my man outside the door says . . . wait for it . . .

Oh yes, you must be the mother of Pearl!

Come on. You can't do that. And this ain't even our *Hey You Can't Do That* moment. Mother of Pearl. I coulda walked out the room on that one.

Hand it to the Brits; so many of their sketches have one of those moments in there somewhere. It's my understanding that John Cleese and Terry Jones were huge fans. They were like, *This is my shit.* The Goon Show? *What is this thing? I want to do that!*

The Goons lit a fire in the imagination of a lot of the Pythons. And that's partially how Monty Python found this signature kind of absurdist/stream-of-consciousness feel that they became famous for. It was at the very least inspired by the fantastic, and fantastical, Goons.

The Pythons also chose to do away with the more traditional revue musical style and instead created a fluid, free-flowing show with their own new and ingenious format. And it was a show with very few beginnings or endings. They pretty much took the audience from one random thought to the next. And, if Monty Python couldn't figure out how to end a sketch, they would just literally say the phrase,

And now for something completely different.

They didn't give a shit. They didn't care. Like, we don't have an ending. Do we have an ending? No. All right. Let's just say the line then. Works for me.

And by the way, here's something else. If there's a weirdness scale that exists for sketch comedy, with something like a 1 being the most normal thing that could happen and 100 being the weirdest thing in the world, when it comes to the comedy of the Pythons, nothing ever would start at a 1. Not even a 14, not even a 57.

For example, their sketch called *The Argument* starts at a solid 86. Now, I know there's way too many sketches to pick from when it comes to the Pythons, but I had to try. So, here it goes.

In this sketch, the brilliant Michael Palin walks into an office to pay for a *service* . . .

> RECEPTIONIST
>
> Oh, yes, sir.
>
> MICHAEL PALIN
>
> I'd like to have an argument, please.
>
> RECEPTIONIST
>
> Well, certainly. Sir, have you been here before?
>
> MICHAEL PALIN
>
> No, no. This is my first time.
>
> RECEPTIONIST
>
> I see. Do you want to have the full argument or were you thinking of taking a course?
>
> MICHAEL PALIN
>
> Well, what would be the cost?
>
> RECEPTIONIST
>
> Yes. It's one pound for a five-minute argument, but only eight pounds for the course of ten.
>
> MICHAEL PALIN
>
> Hm. Well, I think it's probably best if I only start with the one and see how it goes from there.

                              RECEPTIONIST

        Try Mr. Barnard. Room 12.

                            MICHAEL PALIN

        Thank you.

And then he heads down the hallway and knocks on the door. From
inside we hear another gentleman, played by John Cleese.

        Come in.

He opens the door and tentatively steps into the room.

                            MICHAEL PALIN

        Is this the right room for an argument?

                             JOHN CLEESE

        I've [already] told you once.

                            MICHAEL PALIN

        No, you haven't.

                             JOHN CLEESE

        Yes, I have.

                            MICHAEL PALIN

        When?

                             JOHN CLEESE

        Just now.

                            MICHAEL PALIN

        No, you didn't.

                             JOHN CLEESE

        Yes, I did.

It's so stupid. And by stupid I do mean awesome.

```
                    MICHAEL PALIN
    Didn't.

                     JOHN CLEESE
    Did.

                    MICHAEL PALIN
    Didn't.

                     JOHN CLEESE
    I'm telling you, I did.

                    MICHAEL PALIN
    You did not.
```

Then my man behind the desk takes a time-out to ask,

```
                     JOHN CLEESE
    Oh, I'm sorry. Is this the five-minute argument or the
    full half hour?

                    MICHAEL PALIN
    Oh, just the five-minute.
```

What the what? An argument place? Now I don't know about you, but I've never seen anyone pay for an argument. That's definitely an 86 on the 1-to-100 weirdness scale. That kind of thinking, that kind of freedom, inspired generations of sketch artists to think outside of the box.

That's the Way You Like It

After I went to graduate school in the bucolic hills of Happy Valley, Pennsylvania, I went back to the D, the great Motor City, and started looking for work in my chosen profession . . . stage managing. Not kidding. Really. That became my new line of work. Okay. So, maybe it wasn't acting, but it was acting *adjacent*. After all, being in a theater was better than not.

I was also auditioning until thankfully I got an acting job in a show that was called *The Complete Works of William Shakespeare*. And as it was abridged and we were clever youths, the word *works* was spelled W R K S. And William was W L L M. Ah yes, the sight gag, which thankfully works in book format as well as in the case of our clever show.

It was a cool little play done with three actors, where we would perform shortened versions of Shakespeare's plays. We did a read-through of the play one night and it was raucous, it was clever, it was hysterical, and it was . . . unavailable. Seems the managing director of the theater forgot to secure the rights to the play, and another theater nearby had. So we were out in the cold. Not to fear. Our stalwart director created a compilation of scenes, sketches, and songs about the Bard's work.

One of the scenes I performed was a parody sketch called *So That's the Way You Like It*. It was a sketch from the comedy troupe Beyond the Fringe, and it was a blast. And it went something like this:

Get thee to Gloucester, Essex. Do thee to Wessex, Exeter.

Fair Albany to Somerset, must eke out his route.

And Scroop, do you to Westmoreland where shall bold York

Enrouted now for Lancaster, with forces of our Uncle Rutland,

Enjoin his standard with sweet Norfolk's host.

And then he goes on and on with all these other guys' names and telling them what to do. And then finally the speech ends with,

I most royally shall now to bed,

To sleep off all the nonsense I've just said.

It was not only fun to speak the verse, but it was also done at this crazy breakneck speed. I loved all the thoroughly British names. The audiences found it funny. But, if you were a professor of English literature, this shit was hysterical. And somehow, thankfully, after all of these years, it still sticks pleasantly in my memory.

Mike Myers

MOT JUSTE

If there was a periodic table of elements of comedy, one of the elements would be *Pythonium*. And at some point, if you were to look hard enough, you would see that everything I've done has been just an artful or even a straight-up lift of moves and thoughts from Monty Python.

One of the things that I am most inspired by from Python is the idea of *mot juste*: the right words. The right wording. The rhythm of the language. They pay particular attention to language. It's so prevalent that I have to come up with my own term for it which is *mot juste*: the correct wording.

For example: "Here we are with Bill Smith, the head of Soviet relations . . . here we are with Professor Higgins of the Cambridge blah blah blah . . . and here we are with a brown stain, possibly creosote." [To the brown stain] "Brown stain, in your opinion . . ." And it's just a brown stain on a chair, but given the *mot juste* of the setup, of those two guys, before you go "brown stain" . . . it's perfection.

Exactly the words that exist in nature and then to add a twist is everything with British comedy.

Hey You Can't Do That

When I was in graduate school, I went to the movies to see *Sense and Sensibility*. And, yeah, no. You heard that right. And I went to see it by myself, I wasn't even trying to impress a girl or anything. Anyway, in the film there is an actor by the name of Hugh Laurie, and he plays this really dry and dour character. And I thought, *My God, who is that guy?* I mean based on his brilliant performance, he is either the worst person in the world or the most fantastic actor in the world. Thankfully, it turns out he's a phenomenal actor, and also just happens to be a lovely guy. He was also a regular on an old Rowan Atkinson show that I love called *Blackadder*. And on that show, he played this really wide-eyed, super-hyper goofy character that is completely dim-witted. Eventually I put two and two together and realized: *Hey! That's the same guy.* It's part of why I've been such a *huge-Hugh* Laurie fan. Jokes. With words. You know you love it.

And if you're asking, yes, this is the same Hugh Laurie that you might know from the TV show *House*. And more recently he was on *Veep* playing Selina Meyer's (Julia Louis-Dreyfus) love interest, Senator Tom. He's not just a stupendous British actor with a brilliant American accent, he's also a fantastic comedian and an ace at playing the straight man. He can do it all.

Hugh and another fantastic talent (and fellow Cambridge Footlights alum) named Stephen Fry had a sketch comedy show called *A Bit of Fry & Laurie*. The show was delightfully ridiculous and silly, and of course extremely clever. And even though some of their sketches may have been short on the screen, these sons of bitches are sticky and they stay with you for a long time.

This chapter's *Hey You Can't Do That* is one of those blackout scenes. As you may recall, a blackout is a very short sketch that takes a page from the world of burlesque, and is usually just long enough for one joke. And, this short masterpiece comes from Fry and Laurie's Cambridge Footlights days.

Hugh and Stephen are sitting in a pub having a pint . . . and then shit goes down. Hugh Laurie's up here talking 'bout,

Boolee buh blah doobie buh. I shlew-
badee daboo blue blah. I shubadee flew
lad bose. Baa, tooly shoe blawl shula
lad. Bass watu shulee boss shulee. Beh.

Like that's what comes out of his mouth. And Fry is annoyed, stares at him, then sternly says,

Now that's a lot of nonsense and you know it.

BLACKOUT.

A blackout is a very short sketch that takes a page from the world of burlesque, and is usually just long enough for one joke.

And that's it. Wait, what?! That's the whole shopelyblop scene. Nope. Nope. Nope. You certainly can't do that. Okay, y'all can't just be talkin' in nonsense, then BLAM—end of scene. Ain't nobody even talk like that. This bit is so funny to me, and I'm even mad at myself for laughing. But they got me, man. There's nothing I can do about it. It's so stupid. These two motherfuckers got my shit. I can't. I mean, how do you order your drink, brother? I'll take a *bleobyscobey* on the rocks? Sorry, let me try that again: slombie skitty *bloebyscobey* niften dingo bob. And a shalew dee-da-boo to you too.

CHAPTER 7

The Me Generation

In Hollywood, California, on the southeast corner of Sunset Boulevard and Curson Avenue, there used to be a liquor store. Behind that liquor store was a parking lot and a ramshackle two-story house. Almost twenty years ago I lived in that house. Back then it was inhabited by three extremely gracious young men. These saviors of mine provided me a place to hang my hat when I arrived in Los Angeles. And yes, I too was once "that guy."

The generosity of my new roommates was overwhelming, and I always will be thankful to Hayes MacArthur, Ike Barinholtz, and especially Josh Meyers, whose room I got to crash in a majority of the time because he was always at his girlfriend's. Oh, and thank you to Josh Meyers' girlfriend from 2004.

I'm certainly not the first aspiring artist to crash on a sofa on the road to fulfilling a dream. I'm also not the first to do so with the goal of joining the sketch comedy circus. There are many people who came before me, and some even with me, who forged that path. And, in the past thirty years or so, there have been some pretty amazing forgers.

Hopefully you're already fans of Bob Odenkirk and David Cross, Amy Schumer, *The Kids in the Hall*, *SCTV*, Dave Chappelle, the cast of *In Living Color*, and of course the legendary Not Ready for Primetime Players of *SNL*. There are many more of course, and selecting ones to focus on is tough, so I'm going to try to touch on as many as I can.

I'd like to start with one of my heroes: Bob Odenkirk. When I was in grad school, a friend of mine turned me on to *Mr. Show*. At the time, there were already a number of sketch shows out there and they usually followed a certain format. But similar to *Monty Python's Flying Circus*, Bob and his partner, David Cross, agreed that normal needed to get thrown out the window along with any rules that they could find.

Their shows were hilarious odysseys. Sometimes a sketch would end with a character leaving a scene, and they would enter a new scene as a totally different character. A character could also drop something out of the sky in one scene and whatever they dropped would land in another. Or a sketch would finish and they would cut to the inside of a room with people watching the last five seconds of *the previous* sketch on a television set. And then that moment became the beginning of the next sketch. There was a progressive narrative to all of it, and part of the genius is that it's near impossible to guess how the connections would manifest or what was coming. They opened my world to a super cool new set of games I

had never seen before. When I first started watching this show, for me there was a lot of like,

> *Whoa. What just happened? My girl just walked out of that garden party and her husband picked her up, but he's also the guy from the other scene where they smashed all the plates to prove gravity exists . . . ? How are they doing this? And how do I get more of it?*

Every episode was an adventure, and I was on board for it all.

When you go to the movies, there's usually a point where you pretty much know that the bad guy is going to get the better of the good guy, but in the end ('cause it's a movie, and this is how movies work) the good guy is going to win the day. Now, when it comes to Bob and Dave, there was no pattern, or at least not one that was obvious or easy to track. With a Bob and Dave twist, by the end of a sketch the good guy, he may as well have turned into a sandwich of uncooked spaghetti. Anyone who watched the show was fortunate to share in some fun, strange math where two plus two is eggplant.

Anyone who watched the show was fortunate to share in some fun, strange math where two plus two is eggplant.

Yes, in regard to that comedy-heightening math, Bob and Dave are certainly brilliant mathematicians. Thankfully, they weren't the only ones who used a comedy calculator. When I was at The Second City in Detroit, many of my castmates were also exploring connections of different scenes in our shows. For example, there was a scene we did where a drug deal went down in an apartment. One of the drug dealers, in a show of power, aims his gun at the ceiling and he's like, POW POW POW, and shoots up at the ceiling. Three scenes later in the show, there's a sketch where a nurse is removing a bullet from a man's ass and she asks him how he got shot. He tells her,

> *It's the darndest thing. I was in my apartment. I was minding my own business. And then, a bullet came up from the apartment below and it went like right in my butt.*

The cast at The Second City in Chicago, and at the Improv Olympic in Chicago, were on this path as well. We were all working with a similar ethos, and in many ways so was *The Upright Citizens Brigade* and *Exit 57* (these were both shows that were on Comedy Central) and *The State* (which was on MTV). It was a super exciting and explorative time in sketch comedy.

After a few years of grad school, and then a few more years spent honing my craft at The Second City, I headed to the sofas of LA. I was lucky enough to book an acting gig on *Mad TV*. *Mad TV* was a weekly sketch comedy show that was taped in front of a live audience. It was my first big break (as they say) and I was hired as a series regular. It was there I learned how to meet a writing deadline, how to play nice with others, and how to wear high heels.

By the way, Jordan and I didn't meet at *Mad TV*. We met years before in 2003. There was a sketch comedy troupe in Amsterdam called Boom Chicago. At the time, The Second City Chicago and Boom Chicago created an exchange program to spread a little international comedy love. The group from Holland (made up mostly of Americans) made their way to our shores and one of our resident troupes traveled over to their land of free drugs and really good football. (The soccer one.)

Anyhow, we were all abuzz awaiting our European counterparts' arrival. I was hearing whispers from former cast members at Boom about this wunderkind named Jordan Haworth Peele. And yes, that is his middle name. My man's middle name is Haworth. I was also told that this Jordan dude and I had a lot in common. We are both biracial, both came from single parent homes, and we're both ardent lovers of sketch and improv. And I'm gonna tell you right now, he did not disappoint.

I was hearing whispers from former cast members at Boom about this wunderkind named Jordan Haworth Peele.

The Boom show was more improv heavy than most of our Second City revues. They had elaborate setups and frameworks for their improvisations that gave them the context of narrative stories. It was a really impressive way to put a pretty bow on some relatively simple improv sketch games.

> Yes, I was cast in a number of sketches to play a woman, which I found odd for, understandably, a couple of reasons. One of which was that there were a number of women already on the show. And two, unlike Jordan Peele, I really don't make for a very attractive woman.
>
> And yes, Jordan Peele was on the show, and yes, for some reason he looks really good in lipstick. I don't know what it is exactly. I guess it would be his lips, maybe . . . ? Sure, my man has skills for miles, and just also happens to have this cute little nose and some soft features. I don't want to make anybody uncomfortable, I'm just saying he happens to be ravishing when he's in makeup and a wig, and I'm gonna leave it at that.

I recall one of their conceits was a type of Eurovision charity show where Brendan Hunt (from *Ted Lasso*) was in a Bono-esque wardrobe, and he was hosting the event. His cohost was a Danish supermodel named Uta, played by Jordan (wearing an enormous blonde wig and the perfect vapid smile). He made a choice that English was not Uta's first language, or second for that matter.

So, Uta struggled with her words. And every time Bono asked Uta her thoughts on the previous act, she would respond by saying,

Yes . . . uh . . . bee-cauz.

And then she would share some kind of inane response that had little to do with whatever the question was. So, for example, Bono would say something like,

So, Uta, what did you think about the lyrical content in that last song being aided by the artistic sign language? It's profound, right?

And then, Jordan/Uta would be like,

Yes, uh, becauz . . . when you . . . open the mouth, then the hands . . .
will be puddin' the symbols . . . into the air for . . . your head thoughts.
Ant becauz.

And it just got more and more ridiculous from there. It was a fantastic bit. I was in absolute hysterics.

Jordan and I officially met backstage one night before Jordan was about to go on. He offered me congratulations and a "well done" as he had seen our show the night before. He saw me improvise this bit about a guy who had a head wound, but had to fill out a ton of paperwork at the hospital just like everyone else . . .

Shot in the head over here . . . Uh, I think I filled out all the forms.
So, is there any way to expedite me seeing a doctor just because . . .
you know, I was SHOT IN THE HEAD.

Excuse me, Nurse, this pen is out of ink. If I could have another pen.
Just want to hurry up the process . . . you know, because I was SHOT
IN THE HEAD.

So, that night when I watched Jordan perform in the midst of his Uta bit, he added,

Yes, ah, becauz . . . when da heart smiles . . . then you are dancin'
ant . . . you get shot in da head.

And I was like, *What?* Seems Jordan was giving a little elegant tip of the cap to last night's offerings. It was nice because it was his way of reaching out, and it was the beginning of our connection. And we have been connected in some way or another ever since.

A few years later; Jordan and I were both hired at *Mad TV* at almost the same exact time. Our understanding was that we were probably going to have to duke it out against each other for one coveted position in the cast. But Jordan Peele, with his uber tactical and beautiful mind, suggested that we write the lion's share of our scenes together. This way we would become a valuable and inseparable unit, and ideally would both be indispensable.

Ken Jeong
A PLACE IN MY HEART

One of my first credits ever was on *Mad TV*. And I believe it was back in 2003 when I first met Keegan-Michael Key and Bobby Lee, two of the stars of *Mad TV*. Bobby had brought me on as a guest in his sketches. It's still one of my favorite things I've ever done. It was so surreal to go to work in the clinic as a doctor, and then at night I would drive over to Hollywood Center Studios and be in a sketch. It was one of my favorite times. A, to be acting alongside Keegan and Bobby, and then B, just to feel the rush of a crowd in sketches. Which I had never done before, especially on a national level. It's definitely got that *My Favorite Year* quality to it, to me. When I see Keegan, I not only see that he is big star, to me, he's just one of the first people I ever met in comedy. And Keegan and Jordan and Bobby were always so nice to me. And even when I was a doctor, they were very encouraging. Keegan was always like, "Keep at it, buddy!" Everyone on *Mad TV*, with their positive energy, I really credit as helping me enter the world of comedy. So, I have a very fond place in my heart for sketch comedy.

And that's the kind of out-of-the-box thinking you get from a puppetry major at Sarah Lawrence who then moved to Amsterdam, and then to Chicago, to learn sketch comedy writing. And by the way, the puppetry thing, 100 percent true. Jordan Peele studied puppetry. My dude is big on the puppets. He be straight up loving some puppets. And y'all know how much I love the Muppets, so you know that's a compliment from me. I'm like, You go. You do you, dawg. Do the puppets. Do your thing. You want to stick your hand up there and make some art? Do your thringst. Do . . . your . . . *thringst* (as Jordan and I would say). It's Keeganese, don't worry. Ideally, everyone will pick up at least some casual conversational Keeganese by the end of this book. Note to self: Next book should be on learning basic Keeganese. Potential title: *Language Praumpsss*. P-R-A-U-M-P-S-S-S. That works.

> *Note to self: Next book should be on learning basic Keeganese. Potential title:* Language Praumpsss. *P-R-A-U-M-P-S-S-S. That works.*

Besides puppets, Jordan and I soon discovered that we are also both big fans of *heavy game*, which is like game times forty-seven. In a lot of comedic scenes, what makes someone laugh could be something subtle. Maybe it's a grounded turn of phrase that you've heard a bunch of times in real life, or it's a goofy character based on someone who is similar to someone you know. But *game* is when you can clearly see what the characters in the scene are trying to achieve, or what obstacle are they facing they need to overcome.

For example, if the equation of a sketch is:

premise + escalation = sketch

then the game is like the plus sign.

Jordan and I love game, and the heavier the game, the better.

In a way, watching a scene that has a great game is kinda like watching a sporting event. When it comes to basketball, we know that the objective is to score more points than the other team. That's the premise. The way you get the points is by putting the ball into the basket, and by getting around your opponents to do so. That's the game, right? And the more obvious the premise and the game, the sooner we recognize these two creative ingredients, and the more dramatic or insane they are, the heavier the game is.

Since Jordan and I both grew up on a steady diet of sketch shows, like Bob and Dave's *Mr. Show*, and since we had trained in improv, we were very familiar with the effectiveness of this heavy game concept. In fact, on our show *Key & Peele*, there are even entire sketches where the characters are *literally* playing a game.

> *In fact, on our show* Key & Peele, *there are even entire sketches where the characters are* literally *playing a game.*

Comedic sketches that have a game, and also are about a game, are not only fun, but it's easy for the audience to catch up real fast, sometimes, the game is even mentioned in the opening title of the sketch (which is clever, and time efficient).

The Highest Mountain of Comedy

Of course, it would be pretty near impossible to do a book on sketch comedy and not at some point mention the Everest of sketch comedy shows: *Saturday Night Live*.

Saturday Night Live is currently the longest running sketch show on television, was a home and breeding ground for everyone from Chevy Chase to Mike Myers to Cecily Strong, and it's also one of the most coveted places in this business to get a job. To become a cast member on this show has been the aspiration for generations of performers, and for good reason.

In 1975 NBC's *Saturday Night Live* premiered with Chevy Chase, John Belushi, Dan Aykroyd, Gilda Radner, Garrett Morris, Jane Curtin, and Laraine Newman.

The show had rotating hosts, musical acts, and all the sketches a kid of any age could want.

They were originally referred to as the "Not Ready for Primetime Players," and were all pretty much unknowns and they all had a special something to offer. For me, the bravery and brilliant mind of John Belushi had the greatest, most profound effect—from killer bees to The Blues Brothers and everything in between. On the show he played a recurring character as a samurai that always stuck with me. And talk about heightening: he took a silly character and premise and went to fantastical places . . . and I loved them all. In *Samurai Delicatessen*, *Samurai Hotel*, and even *Samurai Night Fever*, John put his heart and soul into every unintelligible grunt. He taught me that there's a path that could be paved with being silly, and daring, and that it's even okay to fall down along the way. He brought so much joy to so many.

As for the rest of the show, there are plenty of docuseries and articles and anthologies and biographies out there that cover *SNL*, so those folks don't need too much of my help; but when it comes to specific sketches about a game that also has heavy game, for us it's worth sharing a few examples and taking that short trip to Studio 8H in Rockefeller Center.

With over eight hundred *SNL* episodes and counting, picking only one or two sketch examples to share is certainly a challenge. But as I've already brought up games with *game*, I'm excited to share with you two of my all-time favorite heavy game/game sketches.

The first one is called *Black Jeopardy*.

Now, see what I mean. The premise and game is literally in the title.

As you may have guessed, the setup is fairly simple as it's a show everyone knows . . . with one small addition to the title. As the audience, we immediately make some assumptions about Black contestants, and Black categories and themes.

But to take it up a level, the brilliant team at *SNL* chose to bring in the very lovely, and very *white*, Tom Hanks to play a contestant on the show named Doug. And if that's not enough, on Tom's head they have placed a very . . . let's say . . . *RED* trucker hat. This wardrobe choice doesn't go unnoticed by the other two Black contestants, or by Kenan Thompson in the Alex Trebek role. Kenan starts by asking Doug,

> HOST
>
> Oh man. Doug. You sure you ready to play Black
> Jeopardy?

> DOUG
>
> They told me a fella can win some money, so let's win
> some money. Get 'er done.

> HOST
>
> Well, I admire your confidence.
>
> Let's see our categories: "Big Girls," "I Don't Know,"
> "You Better," "I'm Going to Pray on This," "They Out
> Here Sayin'."
>
> And as always, "White People."

So, that's the setup. We know what the game is, but what we don't know is where or how the escalation is going to come. And y'all know it's coming.

To start, the two African American women are certainly ruling the board. And then, at some point, you know Doug will have to join the game.

> HOST
>
> The answer:
>
> They out here sayin' the new iPhone wants your
> thumbprint for your protection.

Doug buzzes in! The host calls on him, but certainly with some trepidation . . .

> HOST
>
> Oh, okay, then. Doug.

> DOUG
>
> What is: I don't think so . . . that's how they get you.

The host and the ladies are super surprised.

> HOST
>
> Yes! Yes, that's it! That is the answer!

So, it turns out that even though Doug *isn't* a minority, he's from a world where he has some of the same concerns and he's dealing with some of the same issues. Maybe he's even from a similar socioeconomic background. This way he is able to answer these questions correctly and get them points.

It was all put together so brilliantly that it really stuck with me. Game and all. Oh, I'm sorry, game *in a game* and all.

Okay, so I'm just gonna give you one more bit from this sketch because this is my jam. It's just so good.

> HOST
>
> Okay. The answer here is:
> Skinny women can do this for you.

Doug buzzes in.

> Doug . . . ?

> DOUG
>
> What is: Not a damn thing.

> HOST
>
> Yeah. You got it right! Yes!

> DOUG
>
> My wife, she's a sturdy gal.

Now even the other contestants join in applauding Doug.

> Go Doug! Go Doug! Go Doug!

It's perfectionals. Per-fec-tion-als.

The second brilliant game sketch I'd like to share is called *Meet Your Second Wife*. Any guesses what this one is about? Love this setup. So sticky. The game show premise for this one is a little on the meta side, and it goes something like this:

<pre>
                    ANNOUNCER
    . . . and they may not know it yet, but they're all
    guests of America's favorite new show . . . Meet Your
    Second Wife.
</pre>

And the hosts who are played as a team by Tina Fey and Amy Poehler say,

<pre>
                    HOSTS
    And this is the only show where happily married
    men get a chance to meet the person who will one
    day become their second wife. You guys excited?
    Great. Let's meet our first contestant. Brian from
    Alexandria.
</pre>

And of course, the contestants are all super confused.

<pre>
                    BRIAN
    No, wait. I'm sorry. What is this show now?
</pre>

<pre>
                    HOST
    You'll see. Now, I understand your lovely wife,
    Samantha, is in the audience today. She seems
    great . . . for now. But, Brian, let's meet your
    second wife.
</pre>

And then a young girl walks onstage. Like straight up I'm talking like a twelve-year-old girl walks onstage. And Tina continues,

<pre>
                    HOST
    Brian, this is Hannah. Hannah is currently an eighth-
    grade student at Wellington Middle School, but one
    day . . . years in the future . . . she will be your
    second wife.
</pre>

Mike Birbiglia
THE MEASURING STICK

I have loved so many different comedy sketches over the years but, for me, it always comes back to *Saturday Night Live*. It's like the currency of comedy. It's the thing that people understand . . . the "exchange rate" on *SNL* to other sketch comedy shows. It's the measuring stick.

I think part of the key to the success of the show is arguably the consistency of the show, and that it's on every week. Lorne [Michaels] had said, "We don't do the show because it's ready. We do it because it's Saturday night."

There's so many sketches to highlight I wouldn't want to weigh you down, but here are two that stand out for me. First, Chris Farley and Patrick Swayze playing the Chippendale dancers. If people haven't seen it, the premise is that Chris Farley and Patrick Swayze (who is really handsome, from *Dirty Dancing*) are both auditioning to be Chippendale dancers and Patrick Swayze is a pro . . . and Chris Farley is a mess. Chris Farley is like a terrible dancer, and he's sweaty, and it's like he's gross. It's . . . honestly so gloriously stupid that you can't not laugh at this sketch. You can't not laugh.

There's also the Chris Farley, Paul McCartney sketch for *The Chris Farley Show* where Chris is interviewing Paul McCartney and he's basically, like, "Remember when you were in the Beatles?" And Paul McCartney goes, "Yeah, yeah I remember that," and Chris just says, "Yeah, that was awesome." And it's like that is its whole goal; just putting Chris Farley and Paul McCartney as guests together. According to Chris Rock, and many other people who were friends of Farley, that's what Farley was like. Like the writers bottled this concept of this little sketch idea no matter the person being interviewed. Like there are no questions on *The Chris Farley Show*. It's just compliments, and then there's awkwardness that follows that.

For me it's almost like sports. I was a huge Red Sox fan growing up. And at a certain point, I left the Red Sox and I joined rooting for the *SNL* cast. I went from knowing everything about the Red Sox, to knowing everything about *SNL*. It's not that dissimilar. *SNL* captures the hearts and minds of people in the same way.

Sketch comedy is one of the only art forms where there is an institutional gold standard; which is *SNL*. It doesn't mean that other shows can't be better than *SNL*. I think *Key & Peele* was better than *SNL* in different ways. I think *Mr. Show* was better in different ways. But somehow, we're all still comparing them to *SNL*.

Kevin Nealon

MY FIRST SATURDAY NIGHT

When you get on a show like *SNL* you try to psych yourself up so you're not so nervous for the first episode. I had been doing stand-up in front of audiences, so I was used to audiences being there. I told myself nobody's watching the show at home because the ratings had been pretty bad the year before and Lorne got a whole new cast. So, I told myself it's just the people in the studio audience, and you're used to that so go get 'em. And even though I was kind of nervous, it was working . . . until about five seconds before I was about to go on and Lorne Michaels put his hand on my shoulder and goes, "Are you sure this is what you want?"

BRIAN

Well, that's impossible. I love my wife. She supported
me while I've been writing my novel.

HOST

But what if I told you, in a few years, one of your
novels becomes a surprise bestseller and even optioned
for a movie?

And then, they cut back to Brian and you can see this brother got
the cogs turning in his mind. And then he looks up, and as he has clearly
caught up, he shares,

BRIAN

Um, yeah, yeah. I get it now. I get it.

This motherfucker right here is talking 'bout, "Oh, wait a minute. I
get rich off one of those novels? Oh no, I'm definitely leaving *her*." It's so
good. It's so layered. And you don't have any clue what's coming next. And
I'm telling you whatever does come, it's like the next perfect line. Somehow
every line in this sketch is pretty much
exactly what it should be. And I just love
that you learn seventy-five things about
the contestants and who they are in just
like one line. "Oh, yup. Of course. If I'm
rich and famous, I'm out."

*And you don't have any clue
what's coming next. And I'm
telling you whatever does come,
it's like the next perfect line.*

Bobby Moynihan, Taran Killam, and
Kenan do a bang-up job as the husbands . . . who will be most definitely
sleeping on the couch. And Tina Fey and Amy Poehler carry the scene with
aplomb. The ladies are solid. They hit everything out of the park. Like, blam.
They just be like, *Next line. Next line. Solid double. Blam. Stand-up triple.*

Tina and Amy are out there every day making their own paths and
punching up through that (mostly male) comedy ceiling.

Thankfully, more and more they are in good company. For example,
the very bold, brave, and brilliant Amy Schumer has broken some molds

Aristotle, in his book *Poetics*, writes about storytelling and the importance of things being both unexpected and inevitable. The next time you're watching a sketch you love, or hear a joke that takes you by surprise and sticks with you, see if one of the reasons you love them is because the game, the turn, and/or the punch line is something that is *unexpected* and *inevitable*.

herself. From musical parodies to high-concept sketches, she isn't afraid to show us who she is and she doesn't apologize for it. An example of this is Amy's boy band parody sketch, *Girl, You Don't Need Makeup*. The boys in this sketch, they coax Amy to wash the blush and red lipstick off of her face. But once she does, they start having second thoughts. And then, they do this complete *about-face*. (I said it.) And the whole sketch speaks directly to the double standard society puts on women in regard to their appearance versus their intrinsic worth. It makes an important point and it's really funny as well.

Another one of Amy's sacrifices for the cause is the sketch *12 Angry Men*. In the piece, twelve jurors (with a cast that includes Paul Giamatti and Jeff Goldblum) are locked in a room deliberating a case. We quickly find out that the verdict that hangs in the balance is none other than whether or not Amy is hot enough to be on television. It's brilliant. Brilliant. Sure, there were some female trailblazers before Amy, but she certainly planted her own super special comedy flag.

When it comes to planting flags, the show *Portlandia* is the fantastic creation of Carrie Brownstein and Fred Armisen. They are a wonderful comedy team, and together they write really brilliant and specific setups. There's a great sketch of theirs that really stuck with me. It has a game, and then another game, and well, another. It's called *Put a Bird on It* and like all they do, basically the whole bit is . . . follow the motto . . .

You want to make something better . . . put a bird on it.

And we see them painting birds, and they're slapping bird stickers on things, and they're sewing birds onto everything. So, that's one game right

THE HISTORY OF SKETCH COMEDY

Julia Louis-Dreyfus

PREDOMINANTLY MEN

I went to an all-girls school from third to twelfth grade. And I think the fact of being only with women, I did certain things there, and I excelled in certain areas that I might not have if the school had been co-ed. So, I just assumed certain things, including positions of leadership. That was my experience. And, I think I was a little bit . . . shall we say, ballsier, coming out of that situation. I didn't consider gender when I was getting out there. I just didn't consider it. And I was in a world that was predominantly men. Men were the dominant gender in the comedy universes. Not necessarily in acting, but certainly when it came to doing sketch comedy. It was really male-centric. And I just knew, I just had this kind of confidence, I don't know what to say, it didn't thwart me, I just moved forward. I just sort of naturally did it. Maybe I'm just super ambitious. I don't know. There were a lot of gigs I didn't get, you know, it's not necessarily easy out there. I mean when I was on *SNL*, I didn't make a name for myself at all. But I certainly did learn a lot, that's for sure. It's just like, "Why not? Why can't it be me? That doesn't make any sense, of course it can be me."

there. At one point in time, we see Carrie's sweater and she's got this dramatic bird brooch. And they've invaded a woman's craft store. And then the *second* game comes when they go to play with all the bird trinkets in the store. And Carrie starts blowing on things that have paint on them and they get into Fred's eye. He gets super annoyed.

Ow. My eye. God. Would you please stop blowing on the birds?

As if that weren't enough, then a real bird, like a giant pigeon, flies into the store. And then—this is my favorite game of the sketch—you realize they're *terrified* of birds. They're just like yelling at it,

Get it out! You shouldn't exist!

It's total chaos with multiple games stacked on top of each other. *Portlandia* is super fun on many levels. And even when the show's subjects and the setups are pretty far-fetched, there's still something in each scene that everyone can relate to.

Getting Some Race in the Race

The show *In Living Color* had a huge impact. Sure, it was groundbreaking and had an incredible cast, but it also affected me personally on an additional level because there were a lot of people on the show that, well, look like I do. I think it's fair to say that when it aired in 1990 it was the *least white* sketch show out there.

I also remember this cast vividly because they were doing things I had not yet seen in sketch. David Alan Grier and Keenen Ivory Wayans created the show. Keenen happens to be part of a very funny family and Kim Wayans and Damon Wayans joined the cast as well. Rounding out the team you also had T'Keyah Crystal Keymáh, Kelly Coffield Park, Tommy Davidson, and Jamie Foxx . . . the list keeps going. What I mean by that is this show featured someone who would soon become one of my favorite actors of all time: Jim Carrey. It was on *In Living Color* when people really started to take notice of the undeniable force of Jim. Jim truly is an inspiration, and one of the greatest actors and comedians on the planet.

When it comes to *In Living Color*, there are endless groundbreaking sketches, characters, and commercial parodies. One of my favorites was a movie review show called *Men on Films*. This one has a really simple game. David and Keenen play access cable semi-amateur movie reviewers, and when they got to discussing a movie that they didn't like, they would just in unison throw out a snarky,

Hated it!

And then when they discuss a movie that they both like, they would give it two diva snaps. I was like, Wait, you can do that? I didn't know you can do that. But you can. And they did. And I was absolutely in awe, and I wasn't alone. The multiracial cast of *In Living Color* shared 127 episodes of comic joy with the world, and for that I'm proudly giving them their well-deserved two snaps.

When I was working at *Mad TV* there was another sketch show that was a topic of discussion among the cast and crew on set. And one day after rehearsal, Jordan and I decided we needed to see for ourselves what everyone was raving about. So, we sat down together and watched Dave Chappelle on *Chappelle's Show*.

Wait, you can do that? I didn't know you can do that. But you can. And they did.

I remember that the sketches we watched were solid, and we liked how personable and relatable Dave was. But then something happened that would forever change the way I saw sketch and comedy. A man named Charlie Murphy appeared on the show. (It's not lost on me that two of the most inspirational moments in my sketch comedy history came from two men named Murphy. I want to know what mom Murphy feed these boys for breakfast.)

So, *Charlie* Murphy is standing alone on a set and he's telling a story about Rick James. Rick James was a really popular recording artist in the late 1970s and early '80s. He sang a song called "Super Freak," which was a big, big hit. And he was this super creative funky R&B guy. He was Black, but sometimes had this weird golden hair, like honey-colored hair, that was in curls. He was a strange cat, to put it mildly.

Charlie Murphy was really great in a movie called *CB4*, which is one of Chris Rock's early gems, and it was a fantastic movie. If you're making a list, this is a great movie to have on it. And since we are up to chapter 7, y'all should really be making a list by now.

Anyhow, the setup was that Charlie would tell stories, REAL stories, about Rick James, and how he and his brother, Eddie, would hang out and party with Rick. In between clips of Charlie's simple testimonial to the camera they would then cut away to Dave Chappelle in wardrobe, playing a pretty wild and crazy version of Rick James—right down to the platform shoes and the cornrows.

Dave and Charlie would act out scenes from the stories that Charlie was telling. And the bits were ridiculous. You had these scenarios with fighting, and drugs, and licking ladies in nightclubs. All of it overflowing with badass Rick James chaos.

And then, and this is my shit, they cut to Rick James. I kid you not; they cut to the *actual* Rick James. This motherfucker is now also doing his own testimonial to the camera, and he is *corroborating every damn insane thing that Charlie says about him*. It blew my mind. There was one part where Charlie was telling a story about how Rick had gone to Eddie's house, jumped on a white couch (a very expensive white couch) and Rick had mud on his boots. And Rick was grinding the mud into the sofa and just screaming at the top of his lungs.

And after they show the dramatic reenactment of that, they cut back to the interview of Rick James. My man, Rick James, talking about,

Come on. What am I gonna do? Just jump up and grind my feet on somebody's couch? Like it's something I do? Come on. I got more sense than that.

Then this is my shit. Rick James pauses, and then says matter-of-factly . . .

Yeah, I remember grinding my feet in his couch.

It's like he doesn't even know what else to say about it. Then he shares,

Cocaine is a hell of a drug.

It was the real Rick James. It just blew my mind. And then add to that, Dave's brilliant catchphrase—was just the cherry on top of this delicious comedy sundae.

I'm Rick James, bitch.

Dave Chappelle found a way to turn modern sketch on its head. He used a whole new set of tricks that pushed the edge of what you could do in sketch. Some of the greatest moments in sketch in this century come from Dave's *Chappelle's Show*. And he quickly became the newest member of the Key and Peele hero list. Pushing the envelope of what a sketch could be has been at the top of the Jordan and Keegan goal list for a very long time. And to say that Dave was a comedic god on that front isn't overstating.

There are so many influences, and successes, and talents from the last twenty years or so that, sadly, I can't possibly get through all of them here. But I would like to thank the entire cast of *The State,* point out that almost all of the brilliant scenes on *Reno 911* could be kick-ass stand-alone sketches, and I'm going to add that the sketch world is a richer world thanks to shows like *The Chris Rock Show, The Ben Stiller Show* (featuring a young Bob Odenkirk), and the brilliant but short-lived *The Dana Carvey Show.*

Laraine Newman

THE SEEDS OF *SNL*

When Lorne [Michaels] assembled our cast, Gilda [Radner] and I, and I think Danny [Aykroyd] were the only people hired. And so, Gilda and I watched people's auditions. And Jane's audition just really stood out. She was hosting a hurricane party. The premise was basically that any disaster that could happen to this town, had. And it was a hurricane-themed party. So, we watched these auditions, and in the beginning, before we went on, Lorne thought that a way to get us as a cast to congeal was to do improv at his loft . . . which we only did twice. But I do remember that John had a character that was a really down-to-earth kinda Chicago boy, and I had Sherry the Valley Girl, and we were on a date on a roller coaster. And we also did an improv where we were an alien family, and Danny and Jane were the parents, and I was the teenage daughter . . . and then we never did it again, forgot all about it.

And then we had our first show, and, mind you we all came from a show that was structured in this way (The Groundlings and The Second City). You're onstage in costume, you do your sketch, you run offstage, you change clothes, come back in the dark, lights up, and you go. Which is the perfect training for *SNL*, and we mostly all came from that.

Jim Carrey

OPENING DOORS AND WORLDS

When *In Living Color* came along, Damon [Wayans] knew me from the clubs and we would watch each other at night. He asked me to audition, and I auditioned with like five hundred other people, and I got the show. I thought *In Living Color* was a really revolutionary moment, culturally . . . it was an incredible moment to be part of. It not only opened a door for African American comedy, but it also put me in the position of the parallel universe; the opposite universe where I was the minority in the gang. The most amazing part of it was I was invited to be great. They didn't give a damn who I was or what I looked like. They were interested in if I was gonna be great. If I was gonna "bring it." And they loved it. And I learned so much in so many ways on that show. Some of my best friends still are from that show. It just opened up a world.

For the first three years of *In Living Color* I was the "white guy," and somewhere in the beginning of the fourth year everybody knew my name. Black guys came up to me and said, "Man, I never thought that anybody white was fucking funny, and *you* a funny motherfucker." That was like being knighted to me, you know.

K & P Where You At?

Jordan and I spent a lot of time working together on sketches in a little apartment on Gardner Street, and it eventually paid off. When we were lucky enough to be given the opportunity to set up our own show at Comedy Central, we had already put in years of preparation. And for us, where that *luck* met our *preparation* . . . was a place called *Key & Peele*.

When it came to work, we set some challenging goals for ourselves. One of the higher ones being to figure out how to make a person who is watching the show truly laugh out loud. Or, better yet, how to get them to stand up and walk out of the room—because whatever we just did affected them so much that they couldn't stay in their seat. Or the best: How do we get people, in their house by themselves, to say out loud,

These motherfuckers is crazy. They're crazy. Something wrong with y'all.

A lot of times when you're by yourself watching a show, you're appreciating it, but most of the time, you're not really laughing at it. You know what I mean? You're thinking it's clever, or it's good, but you're not actually like out loud laughing.

When it came down to it, *changing the world with comedy* wasn't as important to us as *making world-class comedy*. That, fused together with our nerdy, almost religious, love of sketch, and who we are culturally and racially in the world, were the main ingredients in the stew that became *Key & Peele*.

In case you wanted to ask the question, *"Hey Key, like, you just be spending all of your time with Jordan Peele?"* Yes, pretty much. Because at this point I had left my sofa-crashing days and moved in with Jordan. He was a really good roommate, by the way, with his leather couch, his anime collection, and his love of video games. His work ethic, his tireless drive, and boundless creative acumen was something I was always in awe of. He was and always will truly be one of my favorite human beings in the entire world.

If you've seen our show, then you know that social issues are extremely important to us. We felt the best way to address them was to write rock-solid sketches. Along the way, we figured out a lot about who we were and our identities.

Not only were we both mixed race, but we also both did a lot of code-switching growing up. Code-switching is when you put forward different aspects of who you are depending on the characteristics of the people you currently find yourself in front of. Just about everybody code-switches.

For example, if I'm walking down the street with Elle having a chat about, I don't know, what to have for dinner, and I get stopped by an older Black man who's a fan, my tone, rhythm, and even pronunciations would most likely change as I interact with him. So, I would be saying something like,

> *Code-switching is when you put forward different aspects of who you are depending on the characteristics of the people you currently find yourself in front of.*

Well, sure, honey. If you want to get some salmon, maybe we should just stop and pick some up on the way home.

And then, the older fan would come up and be like,

Hey man, hey. You're that young brother does that show with the other brother. Yeah. I like your work.

And then, I would be like,

Hey man. Thank you, man. That means a lot to me. A lot to me, man. I appreciate it. Ap-pre-ci-ate. Ya know, hey, we just out here tryin' to do our thang.

Then as he waves and walks past, I turn back to Elle and in my sweet husband voice say,

So, I guess, we could go to the supermarket on 15th, if you wanted to.

They usually have a lovely selection of fish.

Maybe you don't even realize when you're doing it, but when you talk to your grandmother you might say something like,

Oh, Grandma, this food is delicious.

But if you're sitting with one of your friends, ain't no way that's coming out of your mouth. With your friends you'd be like,

This shit's fuckin' tasty, dawg.

And I don't care how cool your grandma is, ain't no way you are out there saying *this shit is fuckin' tasty, dawg* to your grandmother. By the way, if, *if* she is *that* cool, then yo, I wanna meet that chick. We gotta kick it . . . you know what I'm sayin'?

I bring up code-switching because it's one of the many tools Jordan and I use to build sketches on our show. Race is something we certainly have a perspective on, and it's a subject that falls perfectly into the *write what you know* camp.

Race is something we certainly have a perspective on, and it's a subject that falls perfectly into the write what you know *camp.*

The first sketch we did that helped us find some of our identity footing is called *Soul Food*. In this sketch, we play two dudes who are trying to . . . gosh, what's the easiest way to say this . . . *out-Black each other* in a soul food restaurant by ordering what could be considered the Blackest thing on the menu. It starts with items like collard greens and pigs' feet, and it ends up at . . .

Okay. I want a platter of stork ankles, an old cellar door, a possum spine, and a human foot.

This competition came from our desire to define the game as quickly and as clearly as we could. We were always looking for fun and clever ways to create layers in our work and make sketches that were funny in multiple ways at once. One of our credos at the time became that any subject matter can be funny if you approach it the right way.

Chris Rock

BEING PART OF THE AUDIENCE

I was just a kid, I was just taking it all in, I wasn't even judging it. I didn't realize, even at a young age, I didn't realize I wasn't *part of the audience.* Even as a kid in high school, I watched comedy as more of an analytical thing, as opposed to like a pure audience member. I was almost never *in the audience.* You know what I mean? I was like always studying it. I don't think I got into the *actual audience* until Eddie Murphy. You know what I mean? I mean, I wasn't watching it like a critic or anything, but I was kinda studying the stuff before Murphy got there. But now I'm *watching* it. Now I'm enjoying it like the average American.

One of our credos at the time became that any subject matter can be funny if you approach it the right way.

A solid example of "any subject" being funny is our *Slave Auction* sketch. Now, listen, inherently there is nothing funny about slavery. It's horrible. It's one of the worst things in the world. It's fucking bullshit. Even still, Jordan figured out how to write a sketch that was essentially about *vanity*, and the subject of slavery was simply the setting. This was a signature of the work on our show. Sometimes it would mean figuring out the funny first, and then adding an element of social commentary later, if, and only if, it was informing the comedy.

So, in the case of the slave auction, we started the scene with me, Jordan, and one other Black man being led up onto an auction block. The bidding begins and my character's like,

> KEEGAN
> [Under his breath]
> You put that whip down and see what happens.

And then Jordan adds,

> JORDAN
> Straight up, I don't care what plantation I end up on.
> I'm straight up staging a revolt.

The other slave on the block is the only one to get bid on. He gets sold and taken away. To which Jordan and I both kinda shrug our shoulders, like that's fine by us.

> JORDAN
> I mean, good. I'm glad I didn't get sold 'cause I
> don't want to be owned by another human being. Ok-ayy.

And then I follow him with,

> KEEGAN
>
> ```
> Whoever buys me, they better kill me the first day
> 'cause I'mma go buckwild on the whole operation . . .
> Okay.
> ```

All of the gentlemen who are taken up to the stage on Lot A are getting bid on and sold. And nobody has bid on us, like not a penny, and it's really starting to get to me and Jordan. We've gone from being upset that someone wants to sell us as slaves to being even *more upset* that we're being left out.

So, the next guy that gets sold from Lot A is very strong and he's huge and he towers over us. And I'm like,

> KEEGAN
>
> ```
> Okay. Well, you have to buy that dude. It's a no-
> brainer. I mean that guy's huge. Massive individual.
> That's two of me. I mean, anybody would buy him. I'd
> buy that dude.
> ```

And then, Jordan says what I think is the best line in this sketch,

> JORDAN
>
> ```
> My question is . . . how'd . . . they . . .
> catch . . . him?
> ```

And then, the next dude up is super, super skinny, but somehow he also gets bid on and sold.

> KEEGAN
>
> ```
> Um, okay.
> ```

> JORDAN
>
> ```
> Now, see now, that surprises me. It's like, do they
> even know what they're looking for . . . ? It's like
> the whole criteria is a little inconsistent. I mean at
> some point I want to be on Lot A.
> ```

KEEGAN

Can a brother get on Lot A?

And then, finally they bring up a man who is so short he'd make Sonny Bono look like Kareem Abdul-Jabbar. So, Jordan and I, we fist-bump, we say our goodbyes. I'm just like,

KEEGAN

Here we go.

JORDAN

Oh, oh, here we go. It's been a pleasure. Give him hell.

And as you may expect, even this tiny dude gets some pretty competitive bids and he's also taken away. We are dumbfounded. We start complaining, and getting a little louder.

JORDAN

How does that happen? That's not true. That's not true. What you just said, that is not true. How does it happen?

KEEGAN

That's gobbledygook. Okay, that can't be true 'cause what can that dude do? Look at him. What could he pick? A cotton plant is this tall.

I feel bad about what I just said, so I turn to the other guy and then the crowd.

KEEGAN

No offense, brother. I'm just saying. Am I wrong? Is he not short? He's short. But you're actually short in real life in the world.

And of course, then we have now offended everyone. The auctioneer calls *us* bigots and he ends the auction. And we are very upset about this.

> JORDAN
>
> Auction's over? Whoa whoa whoa whoa. Ain't over. It's not over. I'm strong, y'all. I'm very strong. I can sleep in a bucket.

So, now we're pretty much begging them to take us . . .

> KEEGAN
>
> I'm fast. I got stamina. And I know magic.

> JORDAN
>
> My worst quality is I'm a perfectionist.

And then, in a moment of pure improvisation, I added,

> KEEGAN
>
> Did I mention this? Docile. I am agreeable to a fault. You should have seen the dude who asked me to get on the boat when we came over here . . . I just walked right on the boat. No big deal. Never seen a boat in my life.

"I want people to watch the sketches and feel like they're watching the funniest five minutes of a ninety-five-minute comedy movie."

Who creates sketches like this? Who thinks outside the box and turns things on their head, and makes a brother want to call us stupid and walk out of a room? Jordan Peele. That's who. Hey, did I mention I love me some Jordan Peele? I love me some Jordan Peele.

Another aspect of our work came from a shared cinematic love and sensibility. We wanted the show to look as good as it possibly could. Our director, Peter Atencio, once said, "I want people to watch the sketches and feel like they're watching the funniest five minutes of a ninety-five-minute comedy movie." We shot on location as often as we could, and added the best lighting, costumes, and amazing hair. Our Emmy-winning makeup team really did a bang-up job. All of our desires, thoughts, experiences, feelings, and theories came together to create the sketch comedy show known as *Key & Peele*. I will forever be grateful for our incredible crew, our incredible guest cast members, and my incredible and unstoppable partner.

Hey You Can't Do That

You know what? I'm going to share a *Hey You Can't Do That* moment from our show. It's a scene that's near and dear to me, and still when I watch it today, Jordan cracks me the fuck up. The sketch is called *Celebrity*, and in the sketch, we're playing a party guessing game and we're competing against the two women we're both on dates with. It's men against women and it's Jordan's turn to be the guesser, and the clues come from, well, me.

We begin, and my character has a piece of paper in his hand and the timer starts, and I very excitedly give Jordan clues.

KEEGAN

Okay. Okay. This guy. E equals MC square.

JORDAN

Albert Einstein!

KEEGAN

That is correct. That is correct. Okay, this is the
Terminator . . . ?

JORDAN

Arnold Schwarzenegger.

KEEGAN

Yeah, yeah, okay. Yeah, now we're talking 'bout . . .
Are you talking to me? You talking to me!?

JORDAN

Robert De Niro. Robert De Niro.

And then . . . this . . . shit . . . happens:

KEEGAN

Yeah, yeah, yeah, yeah. Okay. Okay. This person
pretends to be straight, but he's really gay.

JORDAN

Me!?

The room goes quiet. Nobody is sure what to do. Everybody stares at
Jordan. And me, his best friend, I'm like trying to pretend like nothing
happened. I'm not sure what to say, so I decide to try to keep playing the
game. So, I'm taking it slow now.

KEEGAN

He is . . . [clears throat] excuse me . . . he is
livin' la vida loca.

Me . . . ?

Huh? Wait, what? I try again.

KEEGAN

He is a Latin pop star . . .

After thinking about it, Jordan is confused.

JORDAN

I'm not a Latin pop star.

KEEGAN

No. No, you're not. It's . . . not you.

I try again, with a new clue.

KEEGAN

He bangs. He bangs.

JORDAN

Oh, Ricky Martin . . . ?

KEEGAN

That is correct.

Phew.

JORDAN

Ah. I wrote that one too.

No, no, Jordan, you can't. Like dude. Twice you can't. I'm 'bout to call him up like right now and tell him, y'all ridiculous. I mean this shit is really a double *you can't do that.* When my man says *Me* is one, and then he takes it to a . . . whole . . . 'notha . . . level when he goes, *I wrote that one too.* You can't do that. No, it's not you, man! Ain't no way you a Latin pop star. Oh my God, Jordan Peele: they broke the mold. He may not be Ricky Martin, but my brother Jordan Peele in the best way is livin' la vida loca.

CHAPTER 8

The Tools and Schools of Fools

There are many important connections between education and art. Sir Ken Robinson, the British writer and speaker, said, "Creativity is now as important in education as is literacy." He's in good company . . . Ben Franklin was quoted as saying, "If a man empties his purse into his head, no man can take it away from him. An investment in knowledge always pays the best interest." And Albert Einstein shared many thoughts on the subject, from "Play is the highest form of research," to one of my all-time favorites: "If you want your children to be intelligent, read them fairy tales. If you want them to be very intelligent, read them more fairy tales."

So, why am I sharing this with you now? Because, I am one of many members of the sketch comedy world who learned to appreciate and hone my craft in the hallowed halls of a classroom.

I was in plays in high school, and even received a Master of Fine Arts in acting. But the room where it all came together was comprised of some lights, a blank stage, and a single bentwood chair.

When I was about fourteen or fifteen years old, I went with my father and stepmother on a road trip from Michigan to Utah. On the long drive I was reading a book written by Bob Woodward. Yes, the same Bob Woodward who, along with Carl Bernstein, broke the Watergate scandal. But no, this wasn't a book on politics or newspapers. It was a book called *Wired*, and it's the biography of one of my forever heroes, John Belushi.

Diving into those pages I learned many things. For example, I learned that being given a Belushi-size gift of creativity can come with challenges. I also learned about partying 'til four in the morning, and about something called a speedball. Let's put it this way: I read about a lot of things a fourteen-year-old boy probably shouldn't be reading about. But one of the most important things I took from those provocative pages was that John Belushi had been part of a magical place called The Second City. At the time I certainly didn't know what a *comedy troupe* was, but I was determined to find out.

John Belushi had been part of a magical place called The Second City.

Some people are born into this world with certain gifts and skills right off the bat, while others maybe have some raw talent, but working with a

THE HISTORY OF SKETCH COMEDY

coach, or getting some swimming lessons in, would make them an even better swimmer. I look at acting school like a large swim class. You can practice breathing, work on your stamina and strokes, but in the end, you really don't have any idea how you're going to do until you take everything you've learned and jump into the pool.

Because of the age we are in, all of the technological advances, and the enormous access we have to social media and online classes, there are seemingly limitless opportunities for someone to watch a thousand videos on a screen and learn a lot about how to do *the backstroke*, or *the butterfly*, or for our purposes, *sketch comedy*. But it doesn't matter how much you watch, or read about it . . . if you ain't in the water, you ain't swimming. You won't even really know if you're going to swim or sink until you find yourself a pool.

When it comes to sketch comedy, and to improv, the way you get that answer is by learning as much as you can, then getting on a stage in front of an audience. Thankfully there are schools that teach sketch that also have massive pools that hold a stage, and lights, and some even have room for hundreds of people to cheer you on.

Back in the 1990s, The Second City of Chicago had been franchised to different cities, and one of them was established in my hometown of Detroit. When I graduated from college, I heard about their open auditions, and I considered going. I even thought—*hey, comedy is something that I feel like I have a facility for*. But, I was also nervous. Like really nervous. I was young, I was awkward, I had been adopted, and I was battling issues of self-esteem and having a hard time figuring out where I fit in.

The bottom line is, I was very concerned I might not get into the program and that the devastation of not being accepted would be so overwhelming, I would probably . . . I don't know . . . maybe fall over and disappear. And I guess I'm sharing this now for anyone who may benefit from a reminder that everyone has fears and insecurities, and at least at that time in my life, facing mine wasn't something I felt I was able to do.

Thankfully, around the same time I was also offered a scholarship to a really incredible theater program at Penn State where I could get a master's degree. Going back to school was the path I chose. So, I packed up and headed to State College. For the next three years I studied and worked really hard and learned some Shakespeare, and some Ibsen, and some mime, along with my beloved commedia.

After grad school, I came back home to Detroit and made some new and like-minded friends and we started a small theater. In that process, I met some members of The Second City. With the support of my new theater friends, and a few years of maturity, and a few years of Molière under my belt, I was finally able to summon enough courage to audition.

The Second City

My education at The Second City Detroit began the moment I entered the theater for my audition. Stepping into the room was thrilling; my journey in sketch comedy and improvisation was beginning. I can still picture the cabaret tables, and the distinct smell of beer in the air, from what I can only assume was consumed by the thoroughly entertained crowds the night before.

I was greeted by a very soft-spoken and kind man by the name of John Hildreth. He was there to oversee the auditions and he and I weren't alone. There were a handful of other people in the room who were there to audition as well. John had all of us go on the stage and do some warm-ups to get our minds and ideas flowing. At some point he asked us to create and explore an environment using our imagination and imaginary props. For this exercise he provided us with the suggestion of a bakery.

A wave of relief came over me . . . I've been to a bakery. I started to think maybe I *can* do this after all. I starting gathering my thoughts . . .

Okay, so . . . bakery. What can you find in a bakery? There's an oven. Good. Keep it simple. Oven.

So, now I'm onstage and I'm standing in front of my *oven*. I mime pulling down the handle on the door and I grab one of those wooden paddle things and very carefully pull out some of my freshly baked bread.

As I turned to set my imaginary bread down on my imaginary counter, I looked around so I could try to interact with the other people.

Now, here's where it got interesting. One of the other men auditioning was standing center stage and he was looking out at the empty theater doing what seemed to be a stand-up routine, and the character he created was telling jokes with a very pronounced lisp.

Oh no, did I have a stroke and miss something? Were we supposed to be doing a different exercise? Perhaps something not bread related? I thought I heard *create a bakery*. I mean, this brotha's out there doing an impression of the mayor of Detroit . . . and I'm over here baking sourdough. After a small panic, I decided to go along with whatever was happening around me, and take this opportunity to try to sell some of my freshly baked bread to my new speech-impeded neighbor.

> *I mean, this brotha's out there doing an impression of the mayor of Detroit . . . and I'm over here baking sourdough.*

I later learned that what John and his coworkers were looking for was someone who not only can make choices in the moment and go with the flow, but *also* someone who can work well with others.

Part of the soul of improvisation is having other people's backs and supporting whatever is happening with the people around you no matter what direction they're heading in, or what stage they're on, or whether or not they are following any directions.

Yes, a bakery was indeed the suggestion, but if someone onstage near me decides it's *Showtime at the Apollo* instead, then y'all know I'm gonna start tapping my foot, or getting out a broom.

I was over the moon when I received a phone call asking me to join the cast. A few days later, and a few years after first reading about it in *Wired*, I began what was one of the most influential times of my career: working as a performer in the pool, and school, of The Second City.

If you're onstage, and you're inspired, there are no limits. Having fun and pushing the boundaries of what you can do with your imagination is key. Of course, being a team player is a huge part of this process.

There's a really fun episode of *The Office* with Steve Carell where his character, Michael Scott, is taking an improv class, and no matter what the suggestions are, he has decided that he needs an imaginary gun for a prop . . . because he is always improvising that he's some kind of action hero. Always.

Like straight up: he decides that every single improvisation thrown at him, and even the ones he joins that are already in progress . . . need a gun. This is very awkward and very funny, but not something I would ever recommend . . . unless of course you're doing an improv *about a guy in an improv class who doesn't want to be a team player*, then of course, by all means.

THE HISTORY OF SKETCH COMEDY

Improvising Written Words

My new job started with some trial by fire. Prior to this time, I had very little improv training, and even less in sketch. I knew from years of watching *SNL* that during the goodbyes at the end of the show, very often the host would thank the writers. I understood that the writers helped create the scripts of comedy gold for the performers, but I wasn't on a show with a crackerjack staff coming up with bits that were catered to me. At The Second City, I had to figure out how to be *my own* writer.

When I think of writers, I think of Ernest Hemingway, or Kurt Vonnegut, someone with a pipe sitting at a typewriter. (And for our younger readers: a typewriter is like a computer that doesn't play movies, or have access to the internet, and you can only use it to create words on a piece of paper. Okay, *paper*. Hm. Paper is made from trees.)

As I was saying . . . at The Second City, the only smoking pipes we had were mimed, and smokeless, and we didn't start our process by writing on a typewriter, or a computer. What we did was "write" sketches with our new officemates by throwing out ideas, creating characters and scenarios, and then we would pull the funniest, and *funnest*, moments from our day and use those pieces to create sketches and eventually combine them to build the show that we would perform in front of an audience.

> *We would pull the funniest, and* funnest, *moments from our day and use those pieces to create sketches.*

We would use a camcorder to tape these shows so we could watch them back and tweak them as we needed to. (A *camcorder* is like a very heavy and complicated iPhone, but you can't use it to call anyone, or play a game, or find the nearest pizza.)

Of course, it was priceless to be able to watch our performances and then pull moments from them that would become the scenes we performed every week. And you know what? Some of those very sketches, from all those years ago, are still being taught and performed today.

Part of our process is creating the environments in which the characters live. I love this part. Sometimes in scenes we would create a room using mime, or what improvisers like myself call "object work." This magical room could have things like furniture, or toys to play with, or bakery ovens. Once a room or setting was established, everyone in the audience and onstage "agreed" where the things in the room were. For example, if everyone agrees we are in a kitchen, and we all agree that there's a table in the middle of the room, if you walked across the stage you would need to walk *around* the table.

We did this one night and one of the actors forgot about our table, and walked right through it. Now, you can't ignore that it happened, as you know everyone else saw it too—so you quickly have to justify why the character walked through the table. In this case I looked over and said,

> *Oh no, Gerald's a ghost! Gerald, can you hear me?! Gerald, have you met with some terrible accident and visited us from the great beyond with a warning!?*

One of the many good things about improvisation is that you can take any "mistake" and turn it around. One of our fearless founders, and the godfather of improvisation, Del Close, was quoted as saying,

> *There are no mistakes, only gifts. No matter what is thrown at you, you can make it work.*

Everything that happens onstage can be a gift for the audience if you let it. It's a process, and every day you find new moments, and come up with new ways of tackling the challenges ahead. There is another saying at The Second City: there are no closing nights, only opening nights, because no show "closes"; the work just keeps transforming into new scenes.

Look, I'm not saying it's easy. After all, it takes a mix of boldness and bravery to just jump

Everything that happens onstage can be a gift for the audience if you let it.

Bob Odenkirk

HAPPENSTANCE

I had this conversation with Del Close and that was a kind of happenstance and we talked for about two hours. I was twenty-one years old and I remember leaving his apartment and I walked out of there going, "I'm gonna try to do this. This feels like this could be fun and I could pull it off." And it was weird because he certainly didn't sit around encouraging me or anything. It's just, his ramble through his career, and it was an encouragement to me to feel like there's always opportunities . . . they go in all different directions. Some of them work. Most don't. But if you just keep going, and keep making different things, *some of them* are gonna work. And that was enough for me.

up and try new things and take risks on a stage, especially in front of an audience. A good friend once told me that *just because something is uncomfortable, doesn't mean it's wrong*. As a matter of fact, I'm learning that being uncomfortable is usually where we grow. Of course, it's uncomfortable to throw caution to the wind and be silly, be energetic, be goofy, and especially be vulnerable when others are watching, but this is truly where the magic happens. And to me, throwing caution to the wind seems to be the only way to write.

One night as our cast was experimenting with new material for an upcoming show, one of my castmates and I walked downstage to start a scene. My partner, a fantastic improviser by the name of TJ Jagodowski, chose to play an upper-crust, blue-blooded inhabitant of the Northeast, and with a thick Boston dialect he shared a poetic memory of fall. I decided that my character would be from a working-class, urban neighborhood. And when my partner was finished sharing his thoughts, I threw out my own response, trying desperately to match the beautiful and rich words of my counterpart, but in my own awkward way.

We were both outside using the action of raking leaves. My object work is *on point* and I can use a rake, and even take a break and do some lean-on-my-rake-miming, like nobody's business.

The sketch went like this:

TJ

Love the fall, huh? The fall. I tell you what, when
I was a little kid there, I'd get a big pile of the
leaves going, you know? And, I'd jump in there, spread
'em all over. Completely defeat the purpose of rakin'.
Then I'd run inside and I'd have some corn chowdeh,
come back outside, and I'd do it all over again.
That's fall, you know? For me . . . that's the fall.

I thought about it for a moment and responded the best I could,

When I was kid, uh, I used to go out the front door of
the projects, and I would walk down the street, and if
there was a leaf on the ground . . .

I would jump on it.

And then, and then after I hurt my butt, I would go
back inside, and have some Chunky soup. [beat] That's
fall.

TJ

Yeah. That's wild. It's, it's . . . it's uh—it's like
we had the same childhood.

KEEGAN

Yeah, it is downright spooky. It is.

TJ

Come fall, I'd uh, I'd head upstairs to the solarium,
you know? And my, my mom would be up there beveling
glass. She was a glass beveleh. My dad would bring
up frames he'd made of mahogany in the workshop. I'd
put the panes in the frames, add it to the solarium,
just stare through the glass and watch the leaves
turn colors. That's fall. You know what I mean? To me,
that's fall.

KEEGAN

Sometimes, my dad and me, we would watch *Mahogany*
starring Diana Ross, and my mama would listen to the
Neville Brothers, or the Bevel Brothers as my aunt

used to say, 'cause she couldn't pronounce the Ns.
She . . . she ain't have no front teeth. She, she
be like, she be like, "Hey, let's go listen to the
Blubbel-Brubbas." Like that. "I would love to hear the
Blubbel Brubbas right now." Yeah, that's fall.

TJ

Yeah, it's . . . it's like you're my brother from
another mother, you know?

KEEGAN

Yeah, it's like you my brother of another color.

TJ

Ah, the fall. Come fall, I'd walk down the end of
the pier, you know? And, I'd roll up my pant legs so
they were like clamdiggers, you know? And, I'd put
my tootsies in the surf, there. Sometimes, the crabs
would come up and nibble on there and I'd have to
be, "Get off of there, you naughty crabs. Get off of
there." I'd sit there reading a first-edition John
Cheever watching the sloops go by. That's fall. For
me, that's fall.

KEEGAN

```
I used to smoke cheeba, when I would be listening
to Sloop Doggy Dogg. And one time when I was with my
lady . . . and she gave me crabs. "Get off of there,
you naughty crabs . . ." That's fall.
```

It was pretty magical how the whole thing came together. I do however remember that while we were in the very middle of the improvisation, I had no idea where the characters were located. I wondered: In what scenario would these two seemingly diametrically opposed men be in the same place, at the same time, and doing the same job? This last element nagged at me. Thankfully, in an inspired touch of brilliance, my partner uttered the final line of the scene:

TJ

```
It is amazing the people you meet in a minimum-
security prison.
```

We call this piece *Rake*. And this simple scene, about two men raking leaves and connecting to each other with nostalgia about autumn, is still taught and performed at The Second City today.

Higher Learning

Even though The Second City is the place where I learned how to do the *backstroke*, over the years, there have been plenty of other places where someone could learn how to dive in. In an earlier chapter, I touched upon the Cambridge Footlights and the Oxford Revue. Both of these schools in the United Kingdom were home to many a trailblazer in the world of sketch.

In the United States there are many higher institutions with some pretty amazing theatrical and comedy programs as well, like Yale and even Harvard. Now, you may not immediately connect Harvard with humor, but trust me, the connection is there. After all, it is at Harvard where you can find The Hasty Pudding Theatricals, the comedy troupe students founded in the late 1700s. Members of Harvard's Hasty Pudding Society included legendary comedic greats such as John Quincy Adams, Franklin Delano Roosevelt,

J. P. Morgan, William Randolph Hearst, and Jack Lemmon, all of whom are known for their contributions to humor and sketch comedy. I heard John Quincy Adams had a rubber chicken. I bet his act was hysterical. Then again, maybe it was a wooden chicken. Great bit, though. Great bit.

Okay, so maybe only *some* of them ended up in comedy, but I mean

really if you think about it, a sense of humor comes in very handy when playing in the political circus. And over the years there have certainly been a number of politicians who not only have an appreciation for comedy but are excited to get into the act. After all, I was in a sketch with Barack Obama, and recently in one with Joe Biden, and they both have great wit and comedic timing.

There are other schools in the United States that are breeding grounds for actors who have become comedy greats. For example, in New York City you have New York University where Billy Crystal, Sarah Silverman, Demetri Martin, and Andy Samberg honed their chops. There's also Juilliard, where comedy legends such as Robin Williams, Christine Baranski, and Kevin Kline ate mac and cheese on the quad. Okay, maybe not a quad, a stoop? I'll go with stoop.

There are also places that, like The Second City, are basically training centers solely dedicated to the art of sketch comedy. There is the Improv

You may not know this, but most of the Kennedy family are known for their practical jokes, and even Ethel Kennedy, who is ninety-four years young, still gets in on the action. And Ethel, my darling, if you're reading this, I am still truly sorry that one of your sons put me up to calling you and pretending to be Barack Obama. And if you're curious, yes I really did this, and yes I had her fooled, and yes she was a good sport, and also yes, she's going to get me back for it.

Olympic in Chicago, and Upright Citizens Brigade in New York, also known as UCB. Amy Poehler, Matt Besser, Ian Roberts, and Matt Walsh were all the founders of this groundbreaking program.

The Groundlings in Los Angeles is also a pretty incredible place to learn sketch from the ground up. It's been around since the 1970s and Laraine Newman, Will Ferrell, Cheryl Hines, Lisa Kudrow, Kristen Wiig, Melissa McCarthy, and the brilliant, brave, and bodacious Jennifer Coolidge are all Main Company alums.

As for me, and my compadres, being part of The Second City is sort of like having been in a comedic military . . . everyone seems to have a rank based on the years and places they "served" and the stages on which they performed. There is an instant camaraderie. For example, a greeting between me and alum Mike Myers could very easily go something like this . . .

Keegan-Michael Key, '97 to '01 reporting for duty . . . Sir, yes sir.

Mike Myers, '86 to '89 Chicago and Toronto, at ease, soldier.

From actors and writers to producers, directors, and showrunners, the distinguished list of graduates of The Second City is pretty extraordinary.

Chris Rock

THERE'S A PLACE FOR THAT?

No Black people went to school for comedy . . . at least no Black people who grew up where I was from.

I didn't know there was a Second City. I was already a stand-up. I was probably twenty-three or twenty-five years old or some shit. It was like, "Huh! There's a place for that?!" I didn't even know it existed. I might not have known it existed until I got hired for *SNL*. That's how otherworldly that stuff is. You didn't even know that shit exists.

Laraine Newman

LINES AROUND THE BLOCK

I would watch the Dean Martin specials and the Bob Hope specials and Johnny Carson and those would have sketches in them too, which were fun. I always loved Karnak. But that's what I knew from sketch. My real introduction to it was doing it at The Groundlings.

We started out as just an improv workshop, and we would have a scene night where people would present stuff they had written, or a sketch that would come out of an improv that they would work on. And it was just friends that we invited to see the shows. And through word of mouth, there just started to be lines around the block. And then the *LA Times* came and reviewed us, and we thought well, "We better get a name." So, then we decided on *The Groundlings.* That first company had Pat Morita (who was later Mr. Miyagi in *The Karate Kid*); Jack Soo (who was on *Barney Miller*); Valerie Curtin (who was Jane Curtin's cousin and Barry Levinson's writing partner); and Tim Matheson, who eventually played the role that was written for Chevy in *Animal House.* So, these were the people in the first Groundlings company.

Just to name a few: Tina Fey, Stephen Colbert, Steve Carell, John Belushi, Harold Ramis, Amy Poehler, Dan Aykroyd, Gilda Radner, Bill Murray, John Candy, Catherine O'Hara, Eugene Levy, Jason Sudeikis, Chris Farley, Jane Lynch, Tim Meadows, Martin Short, Joan Rivers, Alan Arkin, Jack McBrayer, Horatio Sanz, Aidy Bryant, Cicely Strong, and the recently departed and brilliant Fred Willard.

These people are responsible for some of the most memorable comedic characters in the history of cinema and television. The Second City has always been a place where infinite imagination is rewarded. It's where I learned teamwork and hard work. Coming up with ideas for characters and scenes is always a formidable challenge, and The Second City gave me tools, techniques, and tricks that became the foundation I built a career on. It was here I also found the confidence to feel like I was never lost onstage. If I forgot my lines in a play, I knew I could maybe stall a bit, or experiment a bit, and find my way back. There was always a parachute and I learned that parachute was my imagination.

There's a Tool for That

What all of these institutions have in common is for the most part they use the same tools. Kinda like a comedic shop class, it doesn't matter *where* you learn—a hammer is always a hammer, a drill is always a drill, and the thingy with the sandpaper that you use on wood but it spins around for you is always the thingy with the sandpaper that you use on wood . . . you get the point.

And each sketch is unique. They all contain a premise and they usually escalate, but they come in many shapes and sizes. And that's a good thing. Improv and sketch comedy shows should have *variety*, yes (you know all about variety), to keep the audience interested.

Mike Myers
DON'T INVENT, REMEMBER

There are many, many ways for me to get into a character. Sometimes it's just a vowel sound . . . For my character *Linda Richmond*, it's hearing New Yorkers. When I finally got to New York for *Saturday Night Live*, it was saying the word coffee [caw-fee]. And to me, that was, like, just so yummy . . . that it was coffee [caw-fee], daughter [daw-tah], dogs [dawgs], ya know, *no big whup*.

And I couldn't stop talking that way. It all just came from a vowel sound that doesn't exist in my Canadian accent, which is the "aw" sound. Often, I fall upon my training from Del Close where he said, "Don't invent, remember." And you just try to remember stuff from your life. You don't have to make shit up, you just have to notice, remember, and weaponize.

I'm a noticer . . . and things people say that I hear I put into my back pocket. I heard somebody once say, "I really love the acoustical guitar." And I just loved *acoustical* and then that made it a bit *mystical*. And I think I'm slightly cyclical. And that *acoustical guitar* just stayed with me the rest of my life. You know what I mean? And I just finally put it into the show I'm working on right now. It's mostly drawing from people from my life, and my most creative states are times when I'm in a state of receiving and then remembering.

For example, there are a lot of two-person scenes in sketch. But to mix it up, there are a number of different *kinds* of two-person scenes. There's no limit to what you can do, but there are some categories that improvisers pull from that can get you started, or if you've started and get stuck, they can, um, *unstuck* you.

Maybe you'll recognize some of these . . .

There is a type of two-person scene called *one-upsmanship*. This is where the characters compete against each other or have a clear conflict with each other. The Kids in the Hall had a sketch called *Citizen Kane*. In the sketch, Dave Foley keeps trying to remember a movie he saw and as he describes it, his companion, played by Kevin McDonald, realizes it's *Citizen Kane*, but whenever he mentions it Foley says, "No, that's not it." And it escalates from there. Or there is a scene in the film *Bridesmaids* between Kristen Wiig and Rose Byrne where they compete with each other to give the best, most heartfelt toast at Maya Rudolph's engagement party. And it turns into a toast-off of epic and hilarious proportions.

A two-person *transactional scene* could include a server and a customer: like a restaurant worker and a person at the counter, or a clothing store employee and a customer. These scenes usually consist of two people interacting who have no previous relationship. A really fun example of this comes from one of my favorite sketches of all time: the *Parrot* sketch from Monty Python.

In this sketch, a man tries to return a parrot to a pet shop and the owner doesn't want to accept the return, and says there's nothing wrong with the parrot, but SPOILER ALERT, the parrot is dead. Like he's clearly dead and the salesman insists he's asleep. Its lovely.

There's something called the *swing man*—a sketch where one person is constantly off balance and stuck in between two people who are in conflict or competition with each other. Carol Burnett once did a sketch on her show with Lucille Ball where they were competing car rental saleswomen both trying to convince Tim Conway to rent from their company. Tim is the swing in this scene. (Okay, yes, so maybe that's a three-person scene, but the dynamic is between the two salespeople. Maybe we can call that one two-and-a-half.)

And then there's the two-person *peas in a pod* scene. That's a sketch where everyone in the scene enthusiastically shares the same point of view. The *Cheerleaders* sketches on *Saturday Night Live* are perfect examples. Will Ferrell and Cheri Oteri play two cheerleaders who are best friends and love cheerleading more than anything in the world. They are always on the same team. They are quintessential peas in a pod. And the two of them believe all problems, no matter the size, can be fixed with the perfect cheer. I'm sure if you put some thought into it, you can come up with more categories of two-person scenes that you could use as a diving board for a scene. Mike Nichols (who was a member of The Compass Players, the predecessor of The Second City) famously said that every scene is either a fight, seduction, or negotiation. When it comes to sketch you could certainly start with one of those concepts but there's no limit as to where you can go with it once your imagination gets going.

Sketch Bones

Three of the foundational tools for building a sketch (no matter how many people are in it) are the concepts of who, what, and where. These are the bones of a sketch.

WHO: To have a scene, you need people existing in the environment together and interacting with each other.

WHAT: The what is what's happening in the scene that makes you laugh. There's almost always some kind of a problem or conflict to solve in a scene, and how they solve it is usually where the fun comes in.

WHERE: You need an environment for them to interact in.

Three of the foundational tools for building a sketch are the concepts of who, what, and where.

When it comes to *who*, we are really talking about the *creation* of a character. There are many ways of going about this crucial process. Inspiration for characters is truly everywhere. Observing the folks we come in contact with and ways people are unique, and stand out from one another, can be a lot of fun.

Kevin Nealon

HEAR ME NOW AND BELIEVE ME LATER

I always wondered how people like stand-ups came up with characters, and I realized that you see characters every day: on the street, and in restaurants and stuff. Sometimes you overhear voices and conversations. When Dana Carvey, Dennis Leary, and I were on tour the summer of our first season, I was watching Showtime's *Up Close and Personal* about Arnold Schwarzenegger. I called Dana's room and I told Dana, "You have to watch the Schwarzenegger thing, his accent is so funny." So, we both watched it. And for the rest of the tour, we were talking like Arnold. And that inspired us to come up with characters that talk like that. We thought it would be great to have these two bodybuilders who are like so defensive (you know like Arnold is).

> *[Kevin as Schwarzenegger] You know ef you don' theenk that dis is de best routine you could evah have, and if you don' think so den you don't dezeerve to be en the gym.*

So, we just kind of took *that* to the nth degree.

> *Endt ef you don' theenk that we'er da perfect embahdiment of pumpitude then hear me now and believe me laytah . . . we could take yur belt off an we could cause a flabalanch.*

Here are a few examples. We have all had the experience of being at a party and getting stopped by someone who talks very quickly and uses a lot of *words*, but not a lot of *substance* . . .

> So *he told me that he wasn't going to invite Jenny, not Jenny with the y, but Jenny with the* ie, *I like Jenny with the* y, *but now they're both here, well, frankly I don't think you should be friends with anyone who like spells a simple name wrong* . . .

Or maybe you have a cousin who laughs at everything HE says, even things that aren't supposed to be a joke . . . like,

> *Boy that was quite a game yesterday . . . HA HA HA HA. I think it's gonna snow . . . HA HA HA HA.*

Like, bro, what are you doing?

Or maybe you have an in-law who puts complaints and judgments to melodies. (I'm sure you can imagine a sing/song version of the following.)

> *She's gonna regret wearing those shoo-oose . . . You eat that, you're gonna get gaah-ass . . .*

My point is, the simplest way to create a character is by observing the people around you, and noticing how they speak . . . behave . . . walk . . . how fast they talk, what kind of accent they may have . . . or like what part of Long Island they are from, or maybe they're from the South Side of Chicago. And really, this is an easy one, because the resources for character creation are pretty much endless. Your dentist might have a deep, soothing voice. The employee at a grocery store may have a pronounced facial tic. The massive man sitting across from you on the subway may have a particularly high and squeaky voice. All of these observable qualities can be used to create a *who*.

You can also build a character from "the outside in," and what I mean by that, is sometimes I use a prop or something external to create a character. Like a hat or a wig or a fake mustache or a scarf. Figuring out who would wear a certain piece of clothing, or who would use a specific item, can be the inspiration for filling out the story of who your character is.

Another really helpful tool you can use is what's known as a *body line* or *body profile*. How do the people around you hold themselves? What kind of posture do they have? Does someone have a hunched back and stoop over as they walk? Do they stand really tall? Do they take up a lot of space? Is the person sitting next to you man-spreading . . . goodness, I hope not . . . *but* it could be something you use to create a character.

The dynamic between the characters is always unique. I like to ask myself: How does my character physically respond to my environment? How does my character feel about the other people in the scene? Does someone make me laugh, make me fall in love, does my character get too angry too fast *at uppity white students in a school for not pronouncing their names correctly? I'm talking to you, Joe-nathan.*

> *Does someone make me laugh, make me fall in love, does my character get too angry too fast* at uppity white students?

As far as the *what* . . . there are actually two *whats* in a scene. One is the activity that the characters are doing on the stage, like chopping wood, or buying a dress, or working at a concession stand. If an actor has written or improvised a character that's a doctor, then you have a number of options as to what the *what* can be. An examination, a hearing on malpractice, a lecture while doing surgery, writing a prescription . . . But in the midst of this activity—in order for a scene to move forward—the second *what* needs to appear.

And the second *what* is the conflict that develops in a scene.

When you try to achieve a goal and someone or something is in your way, that's the conflict. If you have dreams about what you want to do with your life, and you're planning on going to school, and your mom's upset that you don't want to go to med school like Uncle Mike, no big deal, right? *But* she also holds the purse strings to your college fund. Boom! Conflict. How do you convince her to let you major in what you want at school?

Now, a conflict isn't always a fight or an argument with another person. A conflict can also be the challenge that's presented by an inanimate object. For example, you have put your money into a vending machine and have made a selection. The machine activates, but your item gets stuck. Boom, the conflict has begun:

Now, how do I get this . . . stupid . . . candy . . . out of the goddamn machine . . . I already tried that. Nope. I'm telling you—I hit the side. Really . . . ? Fine. I'll hit that shit again. I'm coming for you B7!

Which brings us to the *where* of it all. The *where* is the environment the scene takes place in. The *where* is the universe or world you create for the characters to exist in, and the world in which the conflict plays out.

Are you in a dungeon, or maybe in the break room at work, or maybe you work at FBI headquarters. You could be at a children's birthday party, or you could be the captain of a ship that's lost at sea.

The *where* can certainly inform the *who* and the *what*.

Maybe you're a pirate, *and* you walk with a limp, *and* you laugh at your own words, *and* maybe your mother didn't want you to be a pirate. No. She wanted you to study biology and be a doctor like your uncle Mike, *and* now you're stuck at sea, *and* the ship has run out of food, *and* everyone has scurvy, *and* you don't know what scurvy is, *and* maybe your mother was right. And she probably was.

I love it when in a scene a character has a direct relationship with the environment of the *where*. For example, if it's freezing in the scene, then maybe that affects the characters. Perhaps they're shivering when they talk, which could lead to something brilliant.

An object you pick up in an environment can inform the scene as well. (Imagine a little Cajun patois for the following . . .)

You know, this particular screwdriver I just picked up is on sale here at Duetant Hardware on Tchoupitoulas Street in the French Quarter . . . This is where I get all my screwdrivers, eh-hem, I mean my "non-alcoholic" screwdrivers . . . if you get my meaning . . . oooh boy, love me some Harry Connick. That boy can play. Bon temps rouler.

Sometimes a place can be overlooked as a source of comedy. But, I can tell you that when I'm in an environment on a set, I always look for opportunities where the *where* may provide some comedy. After all, the *where* is the home for your *whats* and your *whos*. And ideally you have all three working together to build really fun and dynamic scenes.

I always look for opportunities where the where may provide some comedy.

Don't Think Twice

If you are familiar with Mike Birbiglia, then you won't be surprised at the amount of gushing that is about to happen. And if you don't know who Mike Birbiglia is, be prepared to add him to your newly inspired list. Besides being a contributor to *This American Life* and *The Moth*, he turned his one-man show *Sleepwalk with Me* into an award-winning feature film. He's also a *New York Times* bestselling author. And he's a brilliant actor, with turns in *Orange Is the New Black*, *Broad City*, and *Trainwreck*.

Mike Birbiglia is not only a comic genius, a brilliant writer, and an extraordinary director, he is also perhaps the biggest *fan* of sketch comedy I've ever met. Yes, even bigger than I am. He's never missed an episode of *SNL* and for season after season, he would even live tweet thoughtful and supportive analysis of the sketches throughout the broadcasts. Now, that's a commitment.

Yes, sketch comedy is very important to him. It's so important, in fact, that he produced, wrote, directed, and starred in a love letter to the art form: a heartwarming, heartbreaking, heart-filling film called *Don't Think Twice*. I was privileged enough to star in this passion project of his, and I appreciated every uncomfortable and "too-close-to-home" minute of it.

I'm mentioning it here because the script is about an improvisational sketch comedy troupe in New York City whose members have dreams of making it big. And watching this film is like a mini-master-class in improv. And Mike came up with a truly incredible idea, which was to have the cast come to New York a few weeks before shooting . . . to become an actual improv troupe.

We became a close-knit group. We ate our meals together, went bowling together, and rehearsed and improvised together. We even performed live shows. We were called The Commune, the name of the fictional troupe in the script. Mike brought us all together in a way that I've never experienced on a film. It was pure genius. I'm not alone when I say that amount of intense preparation and connection really comes through on the screen for the audience.

I was also inspired by the courage of the two members of our ensemble who had never improvised before: Kate Micucci, part of the great musical comedy duo Garfunkel and Oates, and Gillian Jacobs, part of the amazing sitcom

Community. They threw themselves into the fire with us every day. And every time we hit the stage, we were supported by two of the most talented and generous improvisers I've ever worked with: Tami Sagher and Chris Gethard. And then, of course, there's our fearless leader Mike, who was also on the team and always had our backs.

The simplicity of some of the foundational tenets of improv were illuminated for me in new and fascinating ways. When we finally got to filming, with a handful of live shows under our belt, we were a lean, mean, improvising machine.

Now, if you've seen the movie, I'd like to point out that when you're watching us on camera performing the film's "improv" scenes, they were actually highly scripted, rehearsed, and memorized. The feeling of being one unit was there in the atmosphere though. And because of the camaraderie we had established, and because of Mike's inspired idea,

We were a lean, mean, improvising machine.

we had an easier time making those scenes look more organic and off the cuff. Backstage was magical as well; we would even do traditional warm-up exercises, just like I had done years before at The Second City. It was an incredible experience all around. And for me, I will always be grateful to Mike for reminding me how much I love learning, and love what I do.

Hey You Can't Do That

On the sketch program *Mad TV* I played a character named Coach Hines. Coach Hines was a hypervigilant, super-aggro phys ed teacher with a chip on his shoulder. He looked a bit like an enraged, soup-strainer-moustachioed Ned Flanders, but in short shorts . . . like very short shorts. Did I mention they were short . . . ?

This character was a combination of different traits of a handful of coaches from my youth, mixed in with a few vocal phrasings of an acting teacher I had crossed paths with, and just a hint of Paul Gleason (the actor who played the detention teacher in the movie *The Breakfast Club*).

There were several Coach Hines sketches on the show, and the one I'm going to share with you today is the original . . . the one that started it all. It's called *The Assembly*. And with this sketch I'm going to say that this *hey you can't do that* should really be more like, *really dude, you can't do that. Like seriously. Don't . . . do . . . that.*

For the setup, the *where* is a high school. And for the *what*, the principal is holding an assembly addressing the student body about fights that have been breaking out at the school. He talks at length about how they have a zero-tolerance policy at the school when it comes to violence and bullying.

Throughout his lecture he gets interrupted by Coach Hines (the character, and the *who*, I created). The coach jumps out of his seat to admonish certain students (who we never see on camera) for being disruptive during the assembly.

Every time he would get up, things would escalate. It starts mild enough with . . .

Sentola, I see you. Secure it, son. Secure it. Okay. You wanna talk? We can talk after school at detention. You think you'll like that huh? Then you keep it zipped.

Then as the lecture continues he gets up again . . .

Okay, you know what, Mr. Maggoey? Here's the envelope—and you just pushed it!

I can see you man, night goggles, I can see you! Alright 20-20 right here buddy, 20-20 chief. Okay, you think I don't know what you're doing. You wanna make fun of Mr. Viggo's hairlip you do it after school or I'm going to give you a hairlip that makes Mr. Viggo's look like a cat scratch.

Then to—

There's the line . . . and you just crossed it!

Mr. Joseph Mentz, is the principal's stupid, dull, monotonous voice putting you to sleep, because if I catch you dozing off one more time, one more time, I'm gonna make you sleep for a long long time!

Ya' knock it off, or I swear I'm gonna stab you in the neck with a pencil!

And then this. God help me.

. . . somebody better speak up right now or I swear I'm gonna lock every single one-a you in this building and set it on fire!

This is talking to kids. So, no, for all you teachers and coaches out there . . . No, no, no, *you can't do that!* Let's just say, that's the line and I'm gonna say yeah, *Coach Hines* definitely crossed it.

But man, did I have a blast and learned so much from the experience I had at *Mad TV*, and we came up with some crazy *whos*, *whats*, and *wheres*.

And I promise, I'm gonna stab *nobody* in the neck with a pencil. Not ever. Not even you, Maggoey.

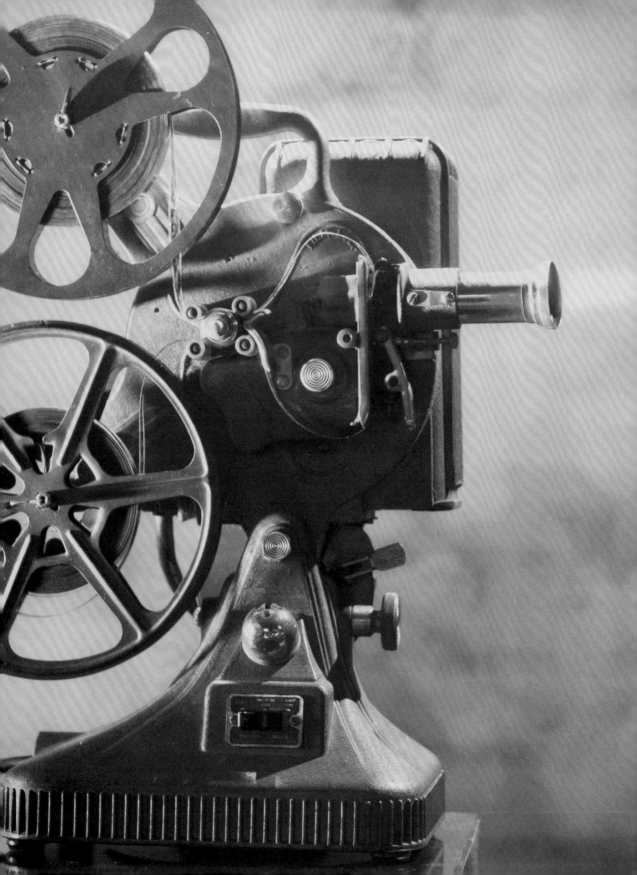

CHAPTER 9

Sketch Goes to the Movies

This chapter is all about the cinema. We tackle where, when, and how sketch movies first started and the path taken along the way. We're going to get into the shorts of the silent era and their connection to sketch. We'll explore movies that are what I like to call *pure sketch films*, and others where the plot is so creatively, well . . . created, that they have built in areas for entire scenes that are basically stand-alone sketches. There are even some movie plots that pretty much exist just so you can do sight gags, short sketches, and wordplay. The world is wide, and we'll cover a whole bunch of them, from some cult favorites, like *The Kentucky Fried Movie* and *Amazon Women on the Moon* to the more mainstream *Airplane!* And then, of course, we touch on the classic: *Monty Python and the Holy Grail*.

I'd like to start with a type of film that was very popular at the turn of the century, the short subject comedy. And again, for clarification, by "turn of the century," I mean the time period when William McKinley was president, not the time period where Reese Witherspoon ran for *class* president in *Election*. Ah, yes, the short subject comedy. A short subject film was a

Gary Oldman

LENNY

When I was a teenager, I would have been about fourteen, I loved the film *Lenny*. Didn't really know who Lenny Bruce was, like, I had a vague idea, but it wasn't until later and I lived here in the US and you get a sense, and you go, "Oh, Lenny Bruce." But the film *Lenny* with Dustin Hoffman doing the routines? I played the record a hundred times 'cause I had the soundtrack to it. There were no DVDs in those days. The only thing you could do was get the record of the film, and it had all the sketches, all the monologues. So, I learned all the monologues. There I was in my room with my record player. It's weird, fourteen, kid living in South London, and I guarantee you I was the only person who could do those routines within thousands of miles of that place.

movie that was about forty minutes or less. In the case of comedy, these short pieces were ostensibly really long sketches in disguise. And some of the greatest comedic filmmakers in history created some of these shorts, from Charlie Chaplin to Buster Keaton.

The legendary comedian W. C. Fields started his film career in a short. His debut was in a movie in 1915 called *Pool Sharks*. If you watch it, I think you would agree that it feels like it has more in common with a long sketch than it does with a feature film. It's about two men vying for the affections of a young woman and they spend the entire time trying to one-up each other. Everything in the movie revolves around this premise. There are no pesky "B" or secondary stories, and we don't explore any other characters or what they may want or need. A short subject film would very often just have one plotline, and they weren't concerned about anybody else or how supporting characters affected the lead or leads.

Once the conflict in *Pool Sharks* is set up, the majority of the film is spent around a pool table where the two gentlemen try to outperform each other with fancy trick shots. And by the way, even though there are trick shots that are created with rudimentary special effects in the film,

W. C. Fields was actually known to be an amazing pool player, as well as a pretty great juggler. I know it's not what most people think of when it comes to W. C., but he truly had a gift for juggling balls and cigar boxes. (The videos are out there and pretty easy to find.) The trick shots in the movie are really goofy and corny, and they're lots of fun. W. C. Fields would hit the cue ball, the cue ball would hit all the rest of the balls, and they would all go into the pockets. Then there'd be a pause, and then the balls would all come back out of their holes and reassemble into the triangle. And you just know that everybody in the theater was calling out,

Huzzah! Oh, great shot!

The special effects were certainly incredible for the time. If you were at the movies watching this, I *can* imagine you'd be like,

Oh my gosh, Bill, did you see that? Put your peepers on this voodoo. Well, what do ya know? That's worth the popcorn alone . . .

Family Business

In the 1930s in the city of New York, there was a woman named Minnie Schoenberg. Her father was a ventriloquist and her mother was a yodeling harpist. What is a yodeling harpist? Maybe exactly what it sounds like, although those are not two sounds I'd ever thought about putting together. Anyhow, Minnie had five children, and four out of five of her sons went into the family business, the business of show. Their names, or at least their stage names, were . . .

Care to guess?

If you answered Harpo, Chico, Groucho, and Zeppo, then you are not only correct, but you are also lucky enough to have had at least some experience with the comedy legend family who called themselves the Marx Brothers.

For a while, they had a very popular stage act that had singing and comedy and music. Their improvisational humor in their vaudeville and comedy revues became the thing they were most known for. It wasn't long after something called *talkies* took to the scene that the Marx Brothers signed a deal with Paramount and took their stage show antics to the big screen. It was a pretty seamless transition for the boys. They would take some of the successful sketches that they did onstage during their shows and string them together with a loose story line, then they would put the whole thing on camera . . . and voilà, it's a movie.

Her father was a ventriloquist and her mother was a yodeling harpist.

I am obsessed with the Marx Brothers. I love the chaos. Ooh, and the way they would poke fun at the upper classes. I always thought it was fantastic whenever there'd be some big, opulent soiree, that the doors would fling open and in would walk Harpo, Chico, and Groucho, and you just knew that some shits was 'bouts to go downst.

The setups were a lot of fun too. The games they played were easy to follow, and the fellas were easy to root for. The wordplay was top-notch as well. Chico would have long bits where he would get words wrong or mix them up in his broken Italian accent. There is one scene in the movie *Duck Soup* where everyone had just found out that there could be a war, and a very concerned and distinguished man says,

Something must be done! War would mean a prohibitive increase in our taxes!

And then right on cue Chico says,

Hey, I've-a gotta uncle who lives in-a Tax-iss.

Of course, the dude is really annoyed by this.

No! I'm talking about TAXES! MONEY! DOLLARS!

And then Chico hits him with,

DOLLAS!? That's where-a my-a uncle lives. Dollas, Tax-iss!

And the best part is that after Chico's line, he and Groucho shake hands. Like these motherfuckers congratulating each other for the joke they just told. That's my jam. It's just complete anarchy. And it's in the movie. It's in the movie. As my partner Jordan Peele would say, *it's . . . in . . . the movie.*

Here's another interesting thing the Marx Brothers did in their movies: they would pause for laughs during a scene. Because so much of their material was previously tested, and perfected, on a stage in front of an audience, they knew where the laughs would be. So, even though they were performing on film, they would still take that pause so that the theatergoers could laugh and not miss the next line. Pretty neat.

Stooges

When I was in junior high, I used to sneak out of my bed and creep downstairs and click on our thirteen-inch black-and-white TV that sat in the corner of the living room. I had to turn the surprisingly loud *on* switch carefully so as to not wake up my parents. The very small set would warm up, and I would turn it to our local channel 50. And this is where I would find reruns of *The Three Stooges.* Then I would call my friend Peter Kuzniar on the phone, and we would spend the next hour with our faces two inches from our respective televisions, watching the antics of Larry, Moe, and Curly, and sometimes Shemp. Poor Shemp was always the fourth Stooge. It's like he was the Pete Best of the Stooges. (If you don't know who Pete Best is, he was the original drummer for the Beatles. And . . . if you don't know the Beatles, they're just one of the greatest bands of all time, and the inspiration for many sketches and even a few "sketch" movies.)

Even before *Saturday Night Live,* my comedic tastes were being shaped by the head bops and eye pokes and face slaps of *The Three Stooges.* And on top of all that slapstick humor (emphasis on the slap), I loved being inundated with their silly puns and their wisecracks. This was my favorite part.

There was a film where the Stooges were masquerading as reporters, and as they check in for an event, they look right into the camera as if it's the point of view of the person checking them in. So, Moe walks up, he looks into the lens, he shows his button, and he says, "Press," and the button says "Press." Then Larry walks up and he has a little pin on his lapel, and he says, "Press," and he walks past. And then Curly walks up, and he's got a button that says, "Pull." It's so stupid. I loved it. Stupid, but come on. Classic.

And then there's this other Stooges bit that still kills me. One of them says to a waiter,

Give me four pieces of burnt toast and a rotten egg.

One of the other Stooges asks,

Four pieces of burnt toast and a rotten egg? What do you want that for?

And the response,

I got a tapeworm and it's good enough for him.

Of course, that's a joke that you would tell in the 1930s because tapeworms I guess were easier to find back then. As for me, thankfully no worms, but I've loved that bit since I was twelve years old. And something that I find fascinating is that they just kept repeating this bit in different movies where the Stooges switched off who said which line. How great is that?

What I didn't realize was, like most people at the time, *The Three Stooges* was my first exposure to comedy shorts. I really enjoyed their fast-paced, energetic, short movies. They grabbed me because they were these bite-size morsels of frenetic fun, and sometimes even today, when I see a short film, I get a memory of my younger self sneaking back into bed after watching the Stooges all those years ago, my comedy mission accomplished.

Taking the Show on the Road

From the 1930s to the 1970s, there were tons of different types of comedy films. There was one category called road movies, where Bing Crosby and Bob Hope would go on an adventure together. There were also some screwball comedies like *Bringing Up Baby* and *Holiday* with Katharine Hepburn and Cary Grant. But there really weren't a lot of sketch movies.

If you ask me, the next big wave of sketch really started with *The Groove Tube* and Woody Allen's *Everything You Always Wanted to Know About Sex* (*But Were Afraid to Ask)*. This is also around the time when the writers Jerry Zucker, David Zucker, and Jim Abrahams created *The Kentucky Fried Movie* and *Airplane!*.

Now, even though both of these Zucker-Abrahams-Zucker movies have a number of truly fantastic, groundbreaking, envelope-pushing, daredevil, jive-talking sketches, the movies follow two different formats. *The Kentucky Fried Movie* is a very rare and special kind of movie, at least in regard to our subject at hand, as it's made up entirely of a collection of sketches. In an anthology, as this movie is, the sketches don't have to necessarily have any connection to each other. There are a handful of other pure sketch movies like *The Groove Tube* and *Amazon Women on the Moon*, but alas, there aren't many of them. *Airplane!*, on the other hand, is a movie with one continuous plot. And even though it has many incredible and comically brilliant stand-alone scenes that fulfill our working definition of a sketch, it's officially a narrative film.

Another great narrative movie that has brilliant scenes that can work as stand-alone sketches is *This Is Spinal Tap*. It was created by Christopher Guest and directed by Rob Reiner. It's a mockumentary about a rock band and their journey. My understanding from Christopher is that they had an outline for the film, but most of the scenes were *improvised* and they just let the cameras roll, and then edited all of these gems together. My

> The Kentucky Fried Movie *is a very rare and special kind of movie, at least in regard to our subject at hand, as it's made up entirely of a collection of sketches.*

Ken Jeong

I DON'T THINK IT GETS ANY BETTER

One of the best movies of all time is *Spinal Tap*. I've seen it so many times. *Spinal Tap.* I still watch it every so often for inspiration, because there is not a false note in that movie. And I'm such a *Spinal Tap* nerd that I watch everything on it. They have like an hour and a half of deleted scenes on the Criterion Collection DVD that I bought twenty years ago. It's basically *another* movie. I watched that over and over again to see the process, and I just don't think it gets any better than *Spinal Tap*.

personal feeling is that just because you improvise a scene doesn't make it *not* a sketch. My belief is, no matter how the scene is created, if it's short in duration, has a beginning, a middle, and an end, has a comedic premise in it, and some escalation, then it constitutes a sketch.

So, yes, I would argue that *This Is Spinal Tap* is chock-full of brilliant *sketches* that are woven in between the concerts and the backstage life of a merry band of *mock*-n-roll heroes. Yes, I said it. Can't stop wordplay. Why would anyone want to? Not me.

Now, on the other hand, a movie like *Midnight Run*, starring Robert De Niro and Charles Grodin (which is one of Elle's and my all-time favorites), has some really, really hilarious scenes in it. And the premises they set up are pretty incredible. There are very funny circumstances that the guys get themselves into, and it's super entertaining. In the middle of the film, our two main characters are stranded in the desert with no money. They pretend to be FBI agents and tell the manager of a local business that someone has been passing counterfeit cash in the area. And they will have to take some of the fake bills back to the lab with them. They do this in order to scam some bills out of his cash register and into their pockets.

Now if you were to watch this scene on its own without knowing *anything* else about the movie, you would see all the components of a sketch.

Christopher Guest

A REAL DOCUMENTARY

In movies which I have directed, whether it's *Waiting for Guffman*, or *Best in Show,* this is *improvisation on film*. I say, "Action," and the scene unfolds. It's a subtle difference, but when you perform onstage it's larger than life, it has to be, because you are performing for an audience that's there . . . when you're on television (even on a sitcom or anything) even though millions of people could be watching, you're performing in front of a hundred to two hundred people (whatever that is). That's why the style of those shows is broad, because you're doing it in front of the audience. You're playing to the audience that's there. You're not playing in the same style as if you were just doing it for *no one there*.

The idea (when we got together to do *Spinal Tap*) was to do something that was subtle, as opposed to broad comedy. So, the perfect thing for us was that when we first showed the movie around, people thought it was a real documentary. They thought this was just a bunch of stupid people in a bad band, you know, or a loud band, or whatever. And so, the idea of being subtle was a thing. But those were not sketches. There were no rehearsals. Because while we wrote the outline for that movie, and created the history of all those bands and ourselves, every scene is improvised on camera.

The scene certainly has a beginning, a middle, and an end. The characters have a goal in mind (to get the tavern owner to give them some money so they can eat). And there are obstacles to their goals to overcome—gaining the trust of the locals and the tavern owner.

And it's fairly short as well. It can exist on its own. Technically, someone could say it is a sketch. But it's funnier when in the context of the rest of the film, and is enhanced by everything we've learned about the lead characters up to this point.

Whereas in *This Is Spinal Tap*, there are many scenes that work as sketches that are funny even if you saw them all by themselves without any other context or backstory or setup needed.

One of the most daring movie sketches I've ever seen in my life was in *The Kentucky Fried Movie*. They created a parody of a TV show from the early '70s called *Thrill Seekers*. So, there's this daredevil and he *doesn't know the meaning of fear*, and he seeks out the most dangerous situations possible to throw himself into. In this bit, we see the daredevil, who is a white dude, and he's dressed in a helmet and this protective gear. He looks a little bit like Evel Knievel. We watch as he walks into the middle of a group of Black men playing a dice game. He looks at the group, then screams the N-word at the top of his lungs and then sprints away. He just runs away as fast as he can. And then the men, who are all enraged by the obscene name-calling, chase after him.

I was in pure shock. It's completely inappropriate, but it was super edgy and really clever. And clearly it made an impression on me because I still think about it all these years later. I was like, wait a second, you can do that? What? What just happened? A man just walked up in there, stood on top of their dice, looked to the heavens, screamed the N-word, and then ran away. I mean, oh my gosh. Well, I guess it was 1977, folks. Okay, maybe that doesn't help. People still do some crazy shit today too. But, like nobody should ever do that. Like ever.

The Groove Tube was another very straightforward sketch film. It stars two young actors who eventually became giants in comedy, Richard Belzer and Chevy Chase. I guess there must have been something in the water because both of these films have a theme about television, film, and commercials, and they both satirize those forms of media. Maybe it has something to do with this time period where television had finally really come into its own, so folks all decided that this was something worth parodying.

Now, when it comes to *The Groove Tube*, other than the theme I mentioned, there are no real connections I'm aware of. The only runners in this case are commercial parodies that are running inside of a news program parody. Other than that, everything's kind of self-contained in this movie.

The Groove Tube has a great commercial parody sketch that I really think is clever; it's about Barbie. The piece starts by showing a doll named Babs with her date, Roy, and then the sketch takes us through all the stages of a relationship with the dolls. So, after the date, it's marriage, then the honeymoon phase, then the doldrums of modern life set in. We see Babs barefoot, pregnant, and doing housework. Then Roy has an affair with his secretary, and it goes on and on like this.

One really great moment happens after the Babs doll discovers that the Roy doll has been unfaithful. We then see them in divorce court with the judge doll. After that, we then see the Babs doll lying on the couch being analyzed by her therapist doll. I mean, hey, this shit happens, folks. It's funny because it's real.

In 1987, a sketch film came out called *Amazon Women on the Moon*. It's another film that parodies television, mostly late-night television and the cheesy B movies that used to air at that time. But the movie does start with a sketch that's outside of the theme. A man (played by Arsenio Hall) comes home from a long day at work, and nothing goes right for him. Like truly nothing. Someone calls him, and it's a wrong number. Someone is asking for Thelma. He hangs up and then he gets a soda from the fridge, opens it, and the soda sprays his face. Then he takes a bite of his sandwich and realizes that it's spoiled so he spits it out. Then, he turns on the garbage disposal to get rid of the sandwich, and his tie gets stuck in the disposal. Then the phone rings, they again ask for Thelma, same wrong number. Then he gets electrocuted, his TV blows up, a bookcase falls on him, and when he's under the bookcase, the phone rings again. And when he answers it, Arsenio utters a line that has stuck in my head ever since. He just goes, "What? Ain't no fucking Thelma here." After a few more expletives, he hangs up the phone with the fury of a madman, and he injures his finger in the process, which leads him to put his foot into a garbage can and he loses his balance and falls out a window.

The pacing and Arsenio's reactions are perfect. And here's the thing; it's a really short piece. It's maybe only around three minutes long, but at the time it felt epic. And I remember watching it with my friend Dave McFarland in their finished basement turned TV room, and we were both howling hysterically. Thelma, great name. Great comedy name.

Now, unlike most of the other movies I just touched upon, *Airplane!* has a plot. A plot is an interrelated sequence of events that move a story along. And what Zucker, Abrahams, and Zucker did, which was super clever, is they made a movie where there was a story that was built to be able to carry all of the sketches. So, if the plot of the film is like a wire hanging from one end of the room to another, then all of the sketches and bits are like the little lights that hang on the wire. And ZAZ, as they were known, hung themselves a long and clever wire with plenty of room for plenty of lights.

Okay. So, maybe some of the sketches in the *Airplane!* franchise were, let's say, more crucial to the telling of the story than others, but they all fit within the theme. If you're a fan of sketch and you haven't seen *Airplane!* or *Airplane II*, I highly recommend you add them to your list. And if you don't have a list yet, I highly recommend you start a list. Come on, folks, we are into chapter 9 here. Y'all should definitely have a list.

Just in case you aren't familiar, the first *Airplane!* movie is about a commercial flight where the men flying the plane get food poisoning, and the only passenger who can save the day is a former military pilot who swore he'd never fly again. Sure, that sounds like a rich, deep, meaningful tale, but it was really just an excuse to create a home for blackouts, wordplay scenes, and physical gags. Basically, the entire script is a home for bits and joke buckets. And in the case of *Airplane!*, that joke bucket may as well be an Olympic-size swimming pool.

This movie truly has everything. There are sight gags, like when the flight attendant is passing out reading material for the passengers, and we cut to a shot of a nun (like in a full-on habit and everything) reading a magazine called *Boy's Life*. Then we cut to a shot of a young boy reading

> If you're an actor or an actress and you're in a comedy, I think you should always be trying to make the crew laugh. If you are not making the crew laugh or making the crew hold back laughter, you ain't doing your job. Like, listen, of course I want to tell the story of the movie, and I want the audience to have a good time, but one of the biggest goals for me is to make the people I'm working with get caught off guard because something is that funny. The crew is usually a, let's say, discerning crowd. Get the crew on your side and you will get a pretty good sense of how well a movie is going to work.

the magazine that he chose: *Nun's Life*. AND on the cover of *Nun's Life* is a nun in her full getup, and she's on a surfboard hanging ten. Double sight gag. It's really great.

And then there are blackouts, like when Leslie Nielsen says,

This woman has to be gotten to a hospital!

And the stewardess says,

A hospital?!? What is it?

And his reply,

It's a big building with patients, but that's not important right now.

Or there's one part where the stewardess says,

Excuse me, sir, there's been a little problem in the cockpit.

And the guy goes,

The cockpit? What is it?

She replies,

It's the little room at the front of the plane where the pilot sits, but that's not important right now.

There are actual "sketches" in the movie, like the one with Barbara Billingsley (who played June Cleaver on the popular TV show from the 1950s *Leave It to Beaver*). Now, let me explain something to you. It's important. *Leave It to Beaver* was the whitest show on television, and I'm talking about in the '50s, and she played the mom on *the* whitest show. So, Barbara in this movie plays a passenger on board the doomed plane, and she tries to assist an ailing man who, like the pilots, has food poisoning. She's the only one on the plane who can help because she's the only person on the plane who can translate for this man. So, the man, who happens to be Black, is sitting on the plane and he starts moaning. He's like,

Ooooh. Uooh.

And the flight attendant goes to him and asks,

Can I get you something?

And my man says,

Man, she mofo butter laying it to the bone. Jackin' me up . . . Tight me.

And the flight attendant doesn't know what to do,

Oh, I'm sorry. I don't understand.

And then the guy's friend adds,

Cutter say he can't hang.

And it's in this moment that June Cleaver gets up to help, and she's old, and she's very white (as I mentioned), and in the sweetest voice she steps up and says,

Oh stewardess, I speak jive . . . He said he's in great pain and wants to know if you can help him.

So, the flight attendant is relieved now,

Oh, all right. Would you tell him to just relax and I'll be back as soon as I can with some medicine?

As the stewardess leaves, June looks at the brother in pain and tells him,

Just hang loose, blood. She going to catch you up on the rebound on the med side.

Then my man is like,

What it is, big mama? My mama didn't raise no dummies. I dug her rap.

And THIS IS MY SHIT, June's not taking it,

Hey, cut me some slack, Jack. Chump don't want no help, chump don't get no help.

And then, as she leaves, this bitch . . . I mean this fine-old-white-woman mumbles,

Jive-ass dude don't got no brains anyhow.

It's amaze balls, with a capital Z.

It's really sublime because a lot of people have been in this kind of situation where there's some foreigner who speaks another language and you're at a loss. But these guys, these motherfuckers are Americans who are speaking jive, but they still need someone to translate. They aren't from another country, but it's as if they're from another country. It's brilliant.

Another sketch movie that follows a linear plot is *Top Secret!*. It's a combination of a parody of a French resistance film from World War II and an Elvis Presley romp. And Val Kilmer, of all

Tracy Morgan

THEN YOU HEAR THE GONG

Blazing Saddles made me want to do comedy. Literally. It made me want to do comedy. Because it was funny. It was poignant. Richard Pryor. Richard Pryor wrote in that movie. He was supposed to star in it, but they gave it to Cleavon [Little]. You can see the different sketches in that whole movie. Punching the horse out. Knocking the horse out. There was a sketch when they started saying, "The Sheriff was a N——!" The way they did that sketch: "The Sheriff was a . . ." and then there was a noise. You didn't hear the word N——. Brilliant. How to write a sketch. How to make it funny. "The Sheriff is a . . ." and then you hear the *gong*. A gong and all of that. It was hilarious. I said I want to be a part of that magic. And I thank the Lord I got on *Saturday Night Live* and learned how to be in a sketch.

people, plays an American rock and roll singer named Nick Rivers who, during World War II-ish, I guess, travels to East Germany for a concert. Once there, he's thrown into a world where he must help a ragtag resistance team save a scientist and maybe along the way win the love of the scientist's daughter. Oh, yes, Master Yoda, the joke bucket is strong with this one. I'm not kidding. You name it, this movie has it. From calling the only Black man in the French resistance *Chocolate Mousse*, to Nick looking for a place to hide backstage at a theater, and he finds the prop room and it's full of airplane propellers and not stage props. Come on! And that's not all. Then he goes to the next door that says "janitor closet." My man opens the janitor closet. There's a janitor up in this bitch. No! And if that wasn't enough, there's a small horse singing. That's right, this horse is singing like a human would sing, and then the horse stops and then this motherfucker coughs, to which the owner shares,

Ya, he caught a cold, and . . . he's just a little horse.

Wait. There's also a motherfucker in this movie named Deja Vu. His name is Deja Vu, and when he is introduced to Nick he says,

Have we met before?

Come on, have we met before?

But, perhaps my favorite moment in *Top Secret!* is when Nick Rivers is in a cell after being imprisoned by our Nazi-esque characters, and he's keeping track of time with chalk lines on the wall. And my man, slowly and with great effort, finishes drawing one of many of his white marks. His talent manager is led into the cell to visit him. Nick looks back at the white lines on the wall, and then with defeat and exhaustion he musters the lines,

Thank God you're here. I've been here . . . twenty minutes already.

No, you can't be talkin' about twenty minutes!

And Val Kilmer is so good at doing all of it. He winks at the lines by overacting some of them, and underacting others. He gives it his all, and it's so good. I mean really? I could have just used bits from *Top Secret!* for every single *Hey You Can't Do That* moment in the book. That's just how crazy awesome *Top Secret!* is.

There are many other films that parody a certain genre and then fill the joke bucket; movies like *Scary Movie*, *Disaster Movie*, and *Meet the Spartans* are all great examples. One of the reasons why they're great is because the genre is right in the title, and you get a sense right off the bat about what you're in for.

Not nearly as famous, although it should be, is *After the Credits*, a short, comedic film from Australia. It is a perfect example of a sketch movie of the short variety. It's just one fantabulous elongated sketch. The short begins with a woman at the airport; she's buying a ticket and rushing to leave the country because the man she loves decided to go through with his wedding instead of following his heart and running off with her, his *true* love. But wait, he DID leave his bride at the altar, and he races to the airport and catches her at the gate just as she's about to board. He shares how much he loves her, and she of course loves him. After they kiss and everyone at the gate cheers for them and everything . . . the credits roll.

BUT WAIT!

The credits rush through super-speed, and THEN the story *truly* begins. To start, as soon as the kiss ends she realizes her checked bag is already on the plane, so she's trying to figure out,

Is there a way I could get my bag off the plane?

And then the woman at the gate is like,

Well, ma'am, we're going to have to delay the flight to do that.

And then all the people that were cheering for them a second ago are now getting very upset,

Oh, come on, man. I've got to be in Kuala Lumpur at six o'clock!

Everybody's pissed,

What the hell are we supposed to do? We're going to dig through the luggage to get your bag?

Then a disgruntled cab driver shows up with airport security and yells out,

There he is. That's the guy. That's the guy that owes me money.

And our in-love dude tries to calm him down,

Well, no, I've told you to leave the cab running.

Of course, he thought this was going to take two seconds, right? Then we find out that in his rush to the gate he left his wallet at the security checkpoint. Of course they're not going to let him have his wallet back. And *then* our couple tries to figure out where they're going to live because he was living with his fiancée, who he was going to marry, and who he just left at the altar.

It just keeps going on and on and on, and it's absolutely brilliant. It's all so unexpected and inevitable, which was a concept created by Aris . . . Aris-to . . . Come on, folks. Once I get to the *to* . . . Aris-to, who else could it be? Aristotle. Good job. Aristotle.

Now, of course we can't do a section on sketch in movies without mentioning Monty Python. I'm gonna say that Monty Python gets extra credit for making two sketch movies with a plot: *Monty Python and the Holy Grail* and *Monty Python's Life of Brian*. And they also made two sketch movies with unrelated material. One was called *And Now for Something Completely Different* and the other was called *The Meaning of Life*. Yes, they're sketch-movie superstars across the board and a must-watch in any book.

Mel Brooks

GOOD FILING

I remember the head of Warner Brothers, I won't mention his name. [Mel immediately mentions his name.] We had a sneak preview of a rough cut of *Blazing Saddles* that was pretty close to what we were going to issue. And he got me into the manager's office with John Calley, who was in charge of the movies there, great guy. They gave me a legal pad and a pencil and said,

> *No farting, take it out.*

> *No punching a horse, take it out.*

> *No hitting an old lady, take it out.*

> *The N-word . . . you can't say that word.*

He gave me so many notes, you know, we would've had a twelve-minute movie if I had listened to all of the things he wanted to cut. He was just appalled at the bad taste that surrounded that movie. So, after he finished, and he left, I crumpled up all the notes and threw them in a paper basket. I remember Calley said, "Good filing." (He was such a sweet guy.)

Anyway, I was very lucky I got final cut for my very first movie. My brilliant lawyer Alan always got me final cut. Even if Warner Brothers wanted to they couldn't fool around with the interior. So, it was all there. And they were very happy with it because it went on to be the biggest picture of the year.

There is a spate of that running around now. "Watch it, bad taste." "Watch it, bad taste." Well, *bad taste* is the solid ground that comedy is made of. I don't think I could have gotten *Blazing Saddles* made now.

Kentucky Fried Teenagers

When I was about twelve or thirteen, one of the kids in my neighborhood invited me over to watch *The Kentucky Fried Movie*, and I had no idea what I was in for. I was just starting on the road to being a fan of sketch comedy at the time, and I had seen a handful of episodes of *Fridays* and *Saturday Night Live* and had even gone to a live comedy revue called Duck's Breath Mystery Theater. But what I was about to witness was *my* first sketch movie. *The Kentucky Fried Movie* is a compilation of commercial, TV, and film parodies. And the introduction to the movie is a newscaster telling the film's viewers that,

> *The popcorn you're eating has been urinated in. Film at 11:00.*

Which, of course, we all laughed at. It was a little bit of a shock to us, but we all thought it was hilarious. This is that perfect example of a runner. Our hero newsman keeps appearing at certain moments throughout the film to give us more silly updates. And I thought it was so clever. I mean, every time we saw him on the screen, there would be this moment of like,

> *Uh-oh, here we go again. What's he going to say?*

We were so excited when he came on the screen. And I savored the anticipation of wondering what ridiculous thing he was going to say next. I also felt like somehow I was in on the joke too. Like they got me, and I'm on team Kentucky. And it had such a huge impact on me. I even remember the last part of the runner that ended the movie with the reporter coming back on-screen one last time. It's still to this day one of my all-time favorite movie lines . . .

> *I'm not wearing any pants, film at 11:00.*

A *runner*, also called a *running gag*, is a recurring theme or joke that builds as time goes on. It's something that you keep coming back to. It can be a setup, place, and character that you revisit at different points during the show. It's not unlike cutting to an image of a ticking time bomb with a digital countdown in a drama, and then you cut back to the action of the movie, and then you cut back to the ticking time bomb. It's a bit that you go back to over and over again. But, ideally, in the case of a sketch movie or comedy, it would be more humorous, unless you're Will Forte playing *MacGruber*. In that case, the runner is funny and, well, *also* happens to be a ticking time bomb. And what's special about *MacGruber* is that it's an actual sketch that someone stretched out into a movie, as opposed to *The Kentucky Fried Movie*, which is a compilation of different sketches.

Hey You Can't Do That

There are many brilliant examples of wordplay from Zucker, Abrahams, and Zucker in their classic *Airplane II*. A couple of times now, we've touched on the concept of a joke bucket. Well, let me explain something to you: *Airplane II* is like the Pacific Ocean of joke buckets. And for this chapter's *Hey You Can't Do That* moment I'd like to share the setup and payoff of one of them.

Now, just about everywhere you turn in a ZAZ film you pretty much know a joke or a visual gag is coming, but if you start a scene by introducing folks with some wacky names, and names that are also very close to the jargon that pilots use, let's say in the cockpit of a plane, well you better put up those tray tables and fasten those seat belts.

The scene starts with one of the pilots speaking to the rest of the team.

                    SIMON

Gentlemen, I'd like you to meet your captain, Captain
Oveur.

                    OVEUR

Gentlemen, welcome aboard.

                    SIMON

Captain, your navigator, Mr. Unger, and your first
officer, Mr. Dunn.

                    OVEUR

Unger.

                    UNGER

Oveur.

                    DUNN

Oveur.

                    OVEUR

Dunn.
Gentlemen, let's get to work.

                    SIMON

Unger, didn't you serve under Oveur in the Air Force?

                    UNGER

Not directly. Technically, Dunn was under Oveur, and I
was under Dunn.

                    DUNN

Yep.

                    SIMON

So, Dunn, you were under Oveur and over Unger.

                              UNGER

    Yep.

                              OVEUR

    That's right. Dunn was over Unger, and I was over
    Dunn.

                              UNGER

    So, you see, both Dunn and I were under Oveur, even
    though I was under Dunn.

                              OVEUR

    Dunn was over Unger, and I was over Dunn.

Nope. Nope. You can't be talking about that Oveur, Unger, Unger
Dunn. Come on, man. You can't do that. You cannot do that. And there
ain't no way all those dudes were working on the same plane at the same
time. That is some shit right there. But it's my jam. I can't stop laughing
at this. It's bad, right? But it's so good too.

I mean, listen, hey, sure, I know folks with silly names. I even know a
dude named Pete Docter, but like he ain't a doctor. That would be fucked
up. You can't just be a doctor named *Docter*. Is Dr. Docter here? Docter?
Docter? Dr. Docter. Oh, God . . . Technically, Dunn was under Oveur,
and I was under Dunn. This motherfucker said, under Dunn. That shit
kills me, and the first time I saw it . . . I was done too. Heck, I was Dunn
and done.

CHAPTER 10

The Best Time to Plant a Tree

There's a Chinese proverb that states, "The best time to plant a tree was twenty years ago. The second-best time is now." The good news is, when it comes to comedy and sketch, most of the seeds and trees were planted tens or hundreds, or even thousands, of years ago. And every day we are reaping their fruit and making some pretty damn fine sketch comedy pies.

I do have some thoughts about where comedy is heading, but unfortunately, I don't have a crystal ball. I do have a magic eight ball, but when it comes to predicting the future of sketch, the response of *ask again later* isn't of much help. By the way, a magic eight ball isn't as off topic as you may think. As a matter of fact, it may have actually been inspired by comedy—*The Three Stooges*, to be exact.

In a short film called *You Nazty Spy!*, there's a scene where Curly and Moe are visiting with a fortune-teller. She has a round crystal ball in front of her with the number eight on it. With some shenanigans, the ball gets knocked over and falls and breaks, and a predictive message comes out.

Which is pretty cool when you think about it, but alas, it still doesn't get us where we're going.

So, where are we going? Well, in the winter of 2013, I was going to Calgary. Did I mention it was winter? Did I mention Calgary? Jordan Peele and I were shooting season one of *Fargo*. There was one warm day, a bright and balmy 15 below Celsius. So, I guess in Fahrenheit, that's a, let's see, carry the one . . . and you add 20 degrees . . . let's just say it was frigid with a capital *F*. Anyway, Jordan and I were having dinner with the brilliant Bob Odenkirk (an incredible sketch performer who also plays Saul in *Better Call Saul*).

Bob was telling us about one of his latest endeavors, executive producing a sketch show called *The Birthday Boys*. It was clear to me now that Bob, who is one of the godfathers of modern sketch, while puttering around in his comedy garden, had started tending to a new crop. Another transition in sketch was taking shape. If the recent generation of sketch includes Chappelle and Schumer, *Portlandia*, *In Living Color*, and *Mad TV*, then what Bob was telling us about is what's next. *The Birthday Boys*, and shows like it, are ushering in a new era.

As far as Bob's show, he became a mentor to the cast. He inspired them to write sketches with solid structure, and he was also crucial in

To give you some context: If the shows from my generation are the *Thomas Guide*, then the new talented group coming up is like GPS. Oh, and for those of you who don't know what a Thomas Guide is, a Thomas Guide was this enormous encyclopedic map book that had every street, every alley, every cul-de-sac in Los Angeles County. It was massive. It was like a Flintstones brontosaurus rib. Remember on *The Flintstones* when they, Fred and Wilma, took that thing and put it on the side of the car? I'm talking about *skwa-blamps*, and like the whole car would go over. That's the shizzit I'm talkin' about. My point is though, we now have GPS—that's the new generation.

encouraging them to explore, and in motivating them to write more, create more, work harder, and work smarter.

Now, this isn't new for Bob. Being fearless and pushing boundaries are some of the traits I have always admired about him and his comedy partner, David Cross. Not only do they have years of experience under their belts, they are also very much like sketch *comedy scientists*: experimenting with different equations to come up with the perfect formula to entertain their audience.

And these geniuses don't care what rules were established. They're like, let's just go and make our own rules. Gravity? Nope. Doesn't apply to us. Sketches need a beginning, a middle, and an end? Nope. We don't even do that. Not Bob and Dave.

We are in an amazing time in history, as far as both technological advances and access to content. When I was a kid, we had a TV with maybe six or seven channels and only three of them actually worked. On the others there was so much static and snow, they looked like Detroit in winter. And today only a handful of people in the industry still use something called film. Most artists use a digital medium. Some just use their phones. When I was a kid, we only had one phone, and it was basically used to *wait* for phone calls . . . and for me to yell at my brother for talking too long to his friends, just in case Terry Perrone might try to call me back.

Today, of course, we have numerous ways of recording, editing, and special effecting videos and content from phones and tablets and computers, even watches. And you know, somewhere out there, some dude gots himself a bionic eye. And y'all know that Terminator asked the doctor to put a camera in that shit.

My point is, there are many ways to create and capture a sketch, and even more ways to share them with the world. And although it can certainly help, you don't really need a studio to distribute it for you. There are many places online, and streaming, that just about anyone can have access to and create and put out their own material. These visionaries used to be called filmmakers, and now they're being called content creators, and it's easy to see how this new world of self-produced videos could influence sketch, and where it's heading.

Kids today have a steady diet of content, the nature of which used to only be found on *America's Funniest Home Videos*, but with so much being captured by these little film studios in our pockets, we are finding what I'm going to call "organic comedy" pretty much everywhere. There's a lot to be said about the joy we get from watching silly dance videos, practical jokes, and people finding any way possible to sink a basketball into a hoop, or for that matter sink just about *any* object into any kind of receptacle.

I mean really, who doesn't love that? Even I'm guilty of it. Like right now, I'm going to take this piece of paper right here, and I'm going to ball it up and let's see. Yeah, okay. Here's what I am going to do. I am going to, behind my back, shoot it off the computer . . . aaaand then it's going to glance off of the table and roll down the hall, then hit the doorframe and then it's going to careen on an angle into that wastebasket all the way back there. So, let's see, here we go.

And I'm talking about . . . blunk, skweech, zing, slaff . . .

He shoots, he scores!

That shot was one in a million, folks! You're not going to see that again. Oh my gosh, that was satisfying. Oh man.

Okay. Well, I'm going to be honest with you. Maybe that shot's *a little* easier to do when just writing about it, but if it *were* online in a video, then blam, I'd have about fourteen hundred million hits right now. You know that's the truth. That would be the situation. Because y'all out here watching some dude maybe take, I don't know, a playing card, and like throw it and cut a banana in half, and you all would click on that a squadrillion times.

So, maybe unlike my super insane complicated masterful trick shot, another aspect that is changing in sketch is (believe it or not) the idea that sketches are becoming less complicated.

Fancy studios and locations and elaborate costumes aren't being used as often because they aren't needed to make most of the homegrown scenes you see today. More and more, it's the comedy that's taking center stage. And sometimes the only stage.

Part of this is from necessity. And part of this is from the *do-it-yourself* mindset of the up-and-coming cast and crew . . . and the budget or lack

Ken Jeong

A PLETHORA OF PLATFORMS

I think that's the beauty of comedy—that it exists on so many platforms. Whether on social media, whether on YouTube, on TikTok. And there's a plethora of platforms to get discovered on now. Like right now, they have the "Please Don't Destroy" guys on *SNL*. And they air those sketches, pre-taped as well as the live ones. And I remember seeing a "Please Don't Destroy" sketch on Twitter; a vaccination sketch that was amazing. And then I saw them on *SNL*, and I was like, "Oh my goodness, look at that. That's beautiful." And they are consistently stealing the show.

I do believe current sketch comedies like *SNL* are a good barometer of where today's comedy tastes fit in. That's the beauty of it now, there are so many ways to be discovered and to get real amazing jobs . . . so many diverse platforms can lead to comedy jobs in TV and movies. There are so many ways to enter the business. And in many ways, it's a meritocracy; if one is funny—one will be discovered. There is something to comedy that is democratic. If someone is really, really funny, people will notice. You can't be denied if you have a true passion and aptitude for comedy.

thereof that the creators have access to. Even with all of the content out there available to us, the cream (as they say) still rises to the top. The most clever and inventive pieces will find an audience. And this rings true, whether you started the next popular dance craze on TikTok or you're The Lonely Island.

The Lonely Island is one of the all-time great DIY sketch troupes. Their members include *SNL*'s Andy Samberg and his partners Akiva Schaffer and Jorma Taccone. And they found viral success online long before gifting body parts to their loved ones (for the uninitiated, I'm referring to their sketch *Dick in a Box*). Their super-creative digital shorts had been gaining popularity and Lorne Michaels, the creator and producer of *SNL*, brought all three of them onboard: Jorma and Akiva as writers, and Andy as a writer and featured performer. Their video *Lazy Sunday* aired on *SNL* and also (like the body-part gift that keeps on giving) became another of their viral sensations. Their tenure saw them create many memorable videos. Most, if not all of them, are in the form of music video parodies about varying subjects like *I'm on a Boat*, and the aptly named *Jizz in My Pants*.

One fantastic Lonely Island special, and a favorite of mine, is a music video they made called *Jack Sparrow*. This expertly done short opens with the boys in a recording studio. And in walks Michael Bolton. Yes, that Michael Bolton. We just love everything Michael says, and he's got that super-cool voice. So, Michael apologizes for being late because he got caught up watching a *Pirates of the Caribbean* marathon. He very excitedly asks if the guys have seen the films, and they say yes. And then Mike says,

Guys, I listened to the new track, and I loved it. And I wrote you this big sexy hook I think you're really going to dig.

And then Andy's like,

Oh, you want to just lay it down?

And Mike gets hyped up,

Boys, let's get to it.

And then the music starts, it's pumping, it's pumping, and we're off. Right? And the boys start getting down in a really edgy and cool night-club hip-hop dance video. And they're rapping about how all the chicks are looking at them, and they got stacks of money, and they're the best at kicking it in the club. And then they get to the chorus and it's Michael Bolton's turn with the hook. And with the most Michael Bolton–esque passionate belt, this motherfucker starts singing about his new hero, Captain Jack Sparrow. Yup. All true. And then we cut to the boys in the recording studio who are looking at each other like,

What? No, that's not right. What's he doing?

And then the song progresses and Michael gets even more detailed about the adventures of Captain Jack. And he does . . . not . . . let . . . up. This dude singing 'bout,

From the day he was born, he yearned for adventure . . .

And of course, the boys groan after every line. And then at one point, my boy Akiva, he just can't take it anymore. And he just calls Michael Bolton out,

Michael Bolton, we're going to really need you to focus up.

That is exactly how he says it. It's really great. So, this is my shit, right? And then Michael straight up responds with,

Roger that, let me try it with another film.

And he starts the next verse with,

Life is a box of chocolates, and my name is Forrest Gump.

To which Andy replies with this perfect deadpan,

Not better.

And then Bolton takes this as a green light to try again. So, then the brother switches to more movies, my man is talkin' 'bout *Erin Brockovich*. Then he goes to *Scarface*. And anyway, it's all amazing. And it's this, and please I'm begging you to forgive me here . . . *out of the box thinking*, yep I said it, that truly sets the bar.

Calling All Colors

Now here, to me, is something that's extremely exciting about what's going on in sketch comedy right now at this time in the twenty-first century: everything is way more diverse than it has ever been before.

For the longest, the longest time, it was just straight up . . . it was just white people, white people, white people, Desi Arnaz . . . white people, white people, white people, Flip Wilson . . . white people, white people, white people, *In Living Color* . . . white people, white people, white people, Dave Chappelle . . . white people . . . me and Jordan.

And all of a sudden it feels like it exploded in the last five years. And that's so awesome, because now we're getting more representation from Black performers. We're also getting representation from LGBTQIA+ performers, from women performers. We've even got representation in the sketch world from *LGBTQIA+ Black women* performers. It's really fantastic.

We're just finally starting to get to a place where we're seeing more perspectives from different types of people in the American landscape. For example, Comedy Central's *Alternatino* is a sketch comedy show that is created by a Guatemalan actor. Guatemalan? My man's name is Arturo Castro. This motherfucker is *Guatemalan*. There is a show right now called *Astronomy Club*, it's an all-Black sketch group, and it has one of the industry's first openly gay Black sketch comedians on television, and they are creating some fantastic content.

Then we have the comedy unicorn *A Black Lady Sketch Show*, whose name says it all. The creator is this bar-setting and ceiling-breaking performer named Robin Thede. She is Second City trained, and was the head writer on Larry Wilmore's *The Nightly Show*. She's joined by Quinta Brunson, who's also an alum of The Second City Los Angeles training center and who created *Abbott Elementary*, and Ashley Nicole Black, who wrote for Samantha Bee's *Full Frontal*.

I've watched many sketches on this show, and I have yet to see a white person. And in the midst of the Black people I've seen, I've straight up only seen, like two Black men on the whole show. Pretty much everybody on the show is Black, and a woman, and it's glorious. The sketches on their show are from a vastly different perspective of the American experience than we usually see. And they do this in very clever ways. They excel at taking what I would call more traditional fare and turn it on its head.

There's this great scene with a couple that's at the altar during their wedding. Robin Thede

Now we're getting more representation from Black performers. We're also getting representation from LGBTQIA+ performers, from women performers. We've even got representation in the sketch world from LGBTQIA+ Black women performers.

is completely decked out in drag. So, she's got cornrows and a full beard, and she's just straight up playing Chris, the groom. And the pastor asks Chris if he takes his fiancée, Lachel, to be his lawfully wedded wife. To which Chris responds with a sly and flirty,

Do I?

And the pastor first responds with a laugh. She's like,

Okay, you're cute.

The answer, son, is I do.

And back to Chris,

Fo sho. Look at it, man. Fine ass.

> THE PASTOR
>
> Nope, sorry. You have to say the phrase
> "I do," just to make it legal.

> CHRIS
>
> Oh, okay. I got you. Ask me again.

> THE PASTOR
>
> Do you, Chris, take Lachel, to be your lawfully wedded
> wife?

> CHRIS
>
> Don't I.
>
> Nope, not quite.
>
> I don't? Just kidding, of course I can.

And then Lachel's like,

> LACHEL
>
> Babe, come on.

The pastor is getting frustrated. They go back and forth with the pastor doing everything she can to finally get Chris to say those two little important words. And after much persuasion, and suggesting that if he *wanna tap that ass* he better say it, she finally gets Chris to say "I do."

And then it's Lachel's turn. And then the pastor's talking about,

> PASTOR
>
> Do you take him for better or for worse?

And my girl is confused and says,

> LACHEL
>
> I mean, does anybody pick "worse"?

                              THE PASTOR

        Okay. For richer or for poorer?

                              LACHEL

        Again, who are these people picking "for poorer"?

The whole sketch is a clever meditation on commitment and the meaning of vows, and it's fresh and brilliant. I've certainly done my fair share of
scenes around the subject of marriage, and I've never seen anything like this.

For these women to be given opportunities not before afforded to
women of color, *and* to watch them nail the material in such a thoughtful
and funny way is thrilling. Truly thrilling.

One of the most inspired sketches on *A Black Lady Sketch Show* aired
during their inaugural season on HBO and it's called *Invisible Spy*. The
sketch revolves around a
super spy named Trinity,
and she's getting orders
for a new mission. So,
Trinity is a plus-size
Black woman. Her "cer-
tain set of skills" is that
she is truly being over-
looked by everyone in
society, and because of
this, she can basically go
anywhere undetected.

At one point in the
sketch, she infiltrates . . . well, she more like just walks right past the security checkpoint in a building. And the security guard, he looks up and sees
she's a heavyset Black woman, then he just goes right back down to his
magazine. And this is how she "infiltrates" the building.

One of the things that is really fantastic is that during the sketch she's
gotta fight another super spy, and they're both, they're like carbon copies
of each other. And in the middle of her fight with this other thick and
beautiful Black woman (played by Nicole Byer) one of them says,

I haven't had to fight like this in years.

And the other one adds,

The last time I fought an assassin, he saw some chick with a long weave down the block—and he just . . .

And they both knowingly say in unison to each other,

. . . wandered away.

What I find so brilliant is that everything they do is based on inside observations made by a group of astute Black women about the issues they face in society, and (in this case) also about how much bias is still out there in regard to a woman's size. And even though most of us are aware that this kind of narrow-mindedness exists, I don't think *this scene* would ever have existed if it weren't created by *this* fearless and talented group of ladies.

Comedy Content Cultivation

Sketch comedy is thriving in this new media world. Today, there are even a number of platforms built to function as a home for short videos and sketches. Websites like Super Deluxe, and Funny or Die, and CollegeHumor came to the forefront and are helping to build this new wave of a comedy boom. A sketch comedian can even get sponsored to make content. While some aspiring voices are pounding the pavement just to get some official industry support by meeting with agents, producers, or managers, others are taking their fate into their own hands and making videos and posting them on YouTube or Vine or TikTok.

A simple sketch, even those done on the cheap, can garner millions of hits online, and new stars are being made every day. For example, there are YouTubers like Julian Smith, who is the genius behind *Hot Kool-Aid*. Now this is a simple sketch that looks like it takes place in the dude's own kitchen. It's all about him persuading his brother to drink hot Kool-Aid. And that's it. That's the whole sketch . . . which got something in the world of thirty million views. No big deal. I mean, the guy is trying to make his brother drink hot Kool-Aid. And that's it. Incredible. Thirty million.

Laraine Newman

ALL THE CURRENT STUFF

I still watch all sketch shows. Of course, I loved *Key & Peele,* I loved *In Living Color*. I like *The Black Lady Sketch Show* and *Baroness Von Sketch*. I like all of it. I see all the current stuff, what the kids are doing. I love that *SNL* has really always been like the Hungry Hippo when it comes to gathering new comedy. I mean, I love the tone and the new voices they seem to have consistently. They always have new styles of writing and performing, as time goes on, and I love that about the show. In terms of tone, it just evolves with the individual perspective of the performers that are of the newer generations. And I love it.

Kevin Nealon

KIDS LIKE TO WATCH IT ONLINE

My son likes to watch *SNL* on YouTube. He doesn't watch it when it's on. All kids like to watch it online the next day or whatever. And I said to him, I said, "Do you ever watch the older versions like Dad was on?" He said, "Sometimes." And I showed him two of my favorite sketches. And he wasn't laughing that much. And I realized that they were very long, the sketches. I think the attention span for audiences is shortening when it comes to sketch comedy. I think sketches are a lot shorter now and maybe even not as joke inspired. It's all about brevity.

And then there's Toby Turner, better known by his stage name (or shall I say screen name) Tobuscus, who has amassed over three billion, with a *B*, hits on his three YouTube channels. A lot of his work constitutes silly little songs and comments on what has happened to him during his day, and humorous and funny observations about video games and pop culture.

There's a group out of Ireland I love, called Foil Arms and Hog, who have been making online sketches since 2008. And out of their modest office in Dublin, they cook up silly and surreal material. They also have some very politically astute sketches. One of my favorite online sketches to date comes from these gentlemen; it's called *U.S. Immigration*. So, to set the scene, two Irishmen are sitting at a desk taking an exam so they can be admitted into the United States. And the officer sitting across from them gives them the lightning-fast rundown, and it goes something like this . . .

                    OFFICER

          Question one . . . The United States is governed by
          two major parties, can you name them?

                    IRISH LADS

          Eh, the gun lobby and big tobacco.

                    OFFICER

          What is the name of America's national holiday?

                    IRISH LADS

          Black Friday.

                    OFFICER

          In what state is the city of Chicago?

                    IRISH LADS

          A state of violence?

                    OFFICER

          What is America's most dominant race?

                          IRISH LADS

The hundred-meter butterfly.

                            OFFICER

Quick-fire round. Finish these sentences. America is
the greatest something in the world.

                          IRISH LADS

Weapons exporter?

                            OFFICER

Martin Luther King had a . . .

                          IRISH LADS

Tough time getting equal rights.

                            OFFICER

Finally, the United States was founded in . . .

                          IRISH LADS

Dubious circumstances surrounding land claims from
Indigenous people . . . ?

                            OFFICER

Welcome to America.

And after all that, the officer right then and there hands them *their
very own gun*. And they're just like, *Yeah, all right, America!* It's fucking
awesome. It's so good.

Of course, many of these short DIY sketches online don't go unnoticed
by the studios. Since many streamers aren't beholden to sponsors, or a lot
of cooks in the kitchen, they can create a vast library appealing to whatever demographic they see fit. And that has made for some fun, fascinating
content over the past few years, with great sketches playing leading roles.

Another standout is the improvisationally based Middleditch and
Schwartz. These bold fellows put out a show where they take a suggestion from the audience and then improvise, with no safety net, for a good

half an hour. What the what? This kind of diving into the unknown, and throwing everything out there, is truly brave and truly brilliant.

A killer show that has found a home on Netflix is Tim Robinson's *I Think You Should Leave*. This is basically an entire sketch show based on how far one can push the comfortability envelope, which is something that Tim does expertly. There are some really inspired sketches on Tim's show, which isn't a surprise. He has a stellar pedigree. He is an alum of both The Second City Detroit and The Second City Chicago main stages, and was a featured player and writer on *Saturday Night Live* before getting his own sitcom on Comedy Central called *Detroiters*. (He created *Detroiters* with his best friend, Sam Richardson, who plays Richard Splett on *Veep*; also a huge talent.)

One of the more, let's say *out there* sketches from *I Think You Should Leave* is called *Has This Ever Happened to You?* It's a commercial parody of one of those malpractice law firm commercials. You know, where their motto is usually: *We'll get you paid*. The sketch starts with Tim standing in front of one of these cheesy law office backdrops that has like forty thousand books on the shelves, and he's speaking directly to the camera and says,

> *Have you been a victim of unfair treatment by a business or a corporation? Has this ever happened to you?*

And then they cut to a video of a man holding two pieces of rotting wood. For the rest of the video we go back and forth between Tim and the dramatization of his narration.

> *Has this ever happened to you? You bought a house and it was not disclosed to you that there was a termite infestation in the walls and in the moldings. So, you have to take it upon yourself to call your own termite extermination company. And when the guys show up, they immediately ask if they can use your bathroom. And for two hours, they take turns going in and out of there, making huge mud pies and over-flushing. And then they go in there together, and you hear a bunch of scrounging around. And then you hear a bunch of yelling. And one of them is standing there and he's shouting at you that his*

friend's foot is stuck in the toilet. And he says, "Help him! You got to help him." And then when you go in to help, he just pulls it out easily. And he laughs because his foot wasn't stuck. It wasn't stuck at all. He was just faking it.

And then they get really serious. And then they say, "It's turbo time!"

And then they both start running around the house as fast as they can and jumping all over the couches. And then you try to jump in and they yell at you and say, "Hey, you're not part of the turbo team! Don't run! You don't run with us! We're the ones who run! Until you're part of this turbo team, walk slowly."

It's so stupid. And by stupid I mean awesome. And I'm sorry, you're not going to see that on a broadcast network schedule these days. You're not. You just aren't.

There are so many other shows out there, and I wish I could touch on them all. So please forgive me if your new favorite show isn't mentioned. Now, if your new favorite happens to be *Reno 911*, you're in luck, *and* I agree with you.

Reno 911 is a brilliant series, and has become popular by being outlandish, bizarre, and entertaining. And it incorporates some of the best aspects of sketch. Oh, I love *Reno 911*. It has a great premise, outrageous and interesting characters, and runners and scenes that are designed to be brief while still packing a punch. And even though *Reno* is a narrative show, almost every scene can be watched as a stand-alone short sketch.

As you've probably figured out, this modern short form really lends itself to a blackout. We discussed blackouts earlier:

the sketches in the burlesque shows that had just one joke in them. That's where they used to bring the lights up on one side of the stage, and a couple of folks would appear, do something funny, and then the lights would go out, and then the lights would come up somewhere else on the stage, and they'd do it again, and again.

Today's version of a blackout is also a short sketch that is, for the most part, the dramatization of a single joke and something that's really easy to pull off and post on today's social media platforms. As far as "the future of sketch" prediction, I'm willing to bet we'll be seeing more comedy with simple setups and themes, and blackouts will become even more prevalent. It might as well be called short attention span theater, and it's super popular and looking like it's here to stay.

I love it when we see people trying to fashion together super-short sketches to make one longer sketch. And who knows, that could even become its own form. Each piece independently funny on its own, but coalescing into a unified and longer whole. The director Jason Reitman used this kind of format for a brilliant homemade version of *The Princess Bride*. He broke up the entire film into shorter pieces that audiences would watch one at a time. And it's so good, it almost doesn't matter what order you watch the scenes in. Not unlike scenes in *Reno 911*, each piece can stand alone and is perfection.

Today's version of a blackout is also a short sketch that is, for the most part, the dramatization of a single joke.

With this format, we're also getting a lot of bang for our buck from character. As an actor, that excites me. If there's going to be a bumper crop of character comedians coming down the pike, I'm all for it. And one of these days, a new version of Wayne Campbell, or Church Lady, or Substitute Teacher will come cascading down from the collective consciousness. Okay, so maybe my magic eight ball can't predict who it will be. But as far as that happening, my ball is saying . . . hmm . . . *you may rely on it.* And that's good enough for me.

DMV Theater

Even though we were a traditional television cable sketch show, so much of the popularity of *Key & Peele* was actually generated online. I remember being stopped on the street by a young lady who told me she had been a fan since the beginning. And as I opened my mouth to thank her, she said, *You know, back when you guys started on YouTube.*

She had no idea that we actually started with a good old-fashioned TV show. Young people are consuming so much content on mobile devices and computers that it never occurred to her that the origins of our show would have come from the *tube* and not *YouTube*. (And for the youngins . . . the tube is what we used to call the television. In the back of it was housed a cathode-ray tube. And no, I don't know what it is or how it worked, but it sounds cool.)

> Jordan and I were writing and designing a show for basic cable on television. You know, like tune in at a certain time on a certain night, sit down and engage in a piece of entertainment for a prescribed period of time. It's literally what people did before there were smartphones. It was called appointment television. Remember Uncle Miltie and folks going to the bathroom at the same time? That was still happening only a few years ago. I guess it happens now on occasion, if you're the Super Bowl or *The Handmaid's Tale*.

Anyhow, this young woman stopping me wasn't the first time I noticed there was a shift in how people might be viewing sketch comedy. No, it was actually at the DMV. Ah, the DMV. I mean, what is the DMV, other than a trial in patience? I'm kidding, actually. I like the DMV. Seriously. I do. I mean, think about it. The DMV is an amazing resource for characters. It's like a subway platform that you wait on for hours, and no train seems to ever come. *But* while you're there, you can collect voices, mannerisms, and other useful and unexpected traits from a wide range of folks you don't usually get to spend quality time with.

So, I'm sitting there and they're currently serving number 26 on the little black screen with the little digital-ass red numbers. And I'm number 29, which is much better than where I was ninety minutes ago, when they were on 112 and these dudes still needed to cycle that shit back through to zero. As I was shuffling through my forms, I hear a familiar voice coming from behind me. I realized the voice was none other than Dave Chappelle. So, I turned around, and instead of seeing Dave, I saw two young brothers huddled over a phone watching a sketch called *The Blind Klansman*. Now if you haven't had the privilege of seeing this sketch, and you've got that list nearby, please put this one near the top. And you should, again, be keeping a list. Folks, this is chapter 10. If you don't have a list, as Coach Hines would say, *I'm going to come over to your house. I'm going to lock you in there and I'm going to set it on fire.* Please forgive him, he's a, um, passionate fellow.

It was in that moment when I realized that sketch had left the confines of our television screens and become portable. Sketch and the convenience of technology had certainly collided. Little did I know that would be my fate as well.

I am looking forward to seeing what the future holds in relation to the DIY mentality of our times. Since just about everyone has a camera, and a sketch can be made from pretty much anywhere . . . who knows, maybe even virtual reality technology could also affect the world of sketch.

Imagine, you could be in the front row of any show you wanted to see, from the comfort of your own home. VR might allow us to even be in a sketch with our favorite performers. Heck, there could be small chips in our brains that let us watch sketches anytime, anywhere, without the need of any other device. Or it might be all of those *and* something else altogether.

But wouldn't it be ironic if all this technology brought us back to the beginning, like all the way back to Ook and Magook . . . or the theater at Epidaurus in Greece. I mean, even *if* there were some kind of virtual reality holographic simulator technology . . . it could end up being just a fancy way to watch a funny scene that has

characters,

a premise,

and escalation.

Jordan Peele

A COLLECTION OF IDEAS

Sketch is such a beautiful art form because it is always evolving and it can take advantage of the way the medium and technology has shifted in a really special way. The problem is sketch is sort of *competing* with the internet; which is sort of curating your content through AI, and sketch is a different kind of curation that just feels like it's rarer and rarer. I mean basically I think sketch is up against Ivan Drago [Dolph Lundgren's character in *Rocky IV*] if you know what I mean. It's up against a real formidable opponent in short form comedy in curation. It's Lorne Michaels vs. YouTube. Tough matchup.

The internet is good at knowing what you want to see next. They've got a highly sophisticated thing going on, but sketch is all about *the thing that you didn't know you wanted to see next*. So, I would think, the only way to really take steps with sketch is with how you choose to curate the sketches that you put together.

I think really, you can't just have one sketch. Sketch kind of is what it is because you have more of them, you have a handful of them. They are what they are *in relation to* each other, you know. This is a collection of ideas you've chosen to present. It's like an album. It's how you think of a real amazing band putting together an album. You've got songs, but each song has to be a masterpiece unto itself. But, when you back up and look at the big picture, it's gotta kinda make a different thing.

Anyone can go anywhere for a funny piece of content right now. But watching them in conjunction with one another, and make them work in that way, is something special.

Hey You Can't Do That

For our final *Hey You Can't Do That* moment, I'd like to share with you one of my favorite sketches of all time. It comes from two of the greatest ambassadors of sketch comedy: Bob Odenkirk and David Cross, and one of the most creative and influential programs in the annals of sketch comedy: *Mr. Show*.

The scene starts with Dave coming in for an audition for a part on a television show. And Bob is playing one of the two producers who are sitting behind a table holding the auditions.

Dave greets them and offers,

                                DAVE

     The monologue that I'll be performing is from the play
     entitled *The Audition*, by Gavin Hollerwood.

The producers make a few jokes about the title.

                          PRODUCERS

     Oh, how apropos.

Then to Dave,

     You can start any time.

                                  DAVE

     Okay.

And he prepares for a moment and then looks up at the producers and asks them,

     Can I use this chair?

They're like,

     Sure. Uh-huh. Yeah, yeah, yeah.

And then Dave stops them, and he's a little frustrated and explains,

DAVE

Oh no, no, no. I started it.

Meaning he started the monologue. So, however odd that may seem, we have all just learned that the first line of the monologue is the question *Can I use this chair?* I mean, the guy already told them that the name of the play is called *The Audition*. Kinda meta, right?

To recap: Dave says,

Can I use this chair?

PRODUCERS

Sure. Uh-huh. Yeah, yeah, yeah.

DAVE

Oh, no, no, no. I started it.

The scene continues from here.

PRODUCERS

Oh God, no. I thought you were asking us to . . .

DAVE

No. No, no, no. I was doing it. I was doing it.

Dave takes a breath and resets.

DAVE

Can, I USE this chair?

And I fucking love this part because then he changes the interpretation of the line. He asks the question (again), and then just stares at the two of them as if he's waiting for a response. And now this is my jam; there is like an eleven-second pause. And both of the producers are totally squirming in their chairs. They don't know what to do. It's extremely awkward. One of them finally gives in and responds,

<pre>
                    PRODUCER
Yeah.

                      DAVE
No! No. No, no.

                    PRODUCERS
Oh God, no, I'm sorry. I am sorry.

                      DAVE
Now just let me, I'll just . . .
</pre>

And now Dave's getting really frustrated. But he composes himself and starts over,

<pre>
Can I use this chair?
</pre>

Crickets.

<pre>
Seriously, can I use it?
</pre>

Crickets.

<pre>
Hello? I need it, for the audition.
</pre>

And of course, now the guys, they're real cautious. Dave keeps going,

<pre>
Could somebody answer me?
</pre>

The producers stand firm. Like they're not going to fall for this shit again.

<pre>
Jesus, talk to me.
</pre>

The guys can't help it.

<pre>
                    PRODUCERS
Yeah. Yeah, fine.
</pre>

```
                        DAVE

    Noooo!


Dave yells at them again, and of course they're sorry again. You can
see they're like, *oh my God, okay, we're going to get it this time.*
    So Dave goes back to square one.

                        DAVE

    Seriously, can I use it? I need it for the audition.

    Can somebody answer me?

    Jesus, talk to me.


It just keeps heightening and heightening; and thankfully for us, so
does the frustration. Even we buy that Dave is addressing them. He goes
on to plead,

    I'm a human being up here, for God's sake.

    Don't just look at each other, answer me!!!

    Can I use it?!!

                      PRODUCERS

    Yes!

                        DAVE

    NO!


And that's awesome, because on his line they actually had just looked
at each other.

                      PRODUCERS

    Are you kidding me with that? That's in there?!?!
    "Don't just look at each other"?

                        DAVE

    Yes.
```

```
. . . exactly when we did it?
```

And my man says my favorite line in the sketch, my man Dave says,

```
                        DAVE

    Yes. It's a good play.
```

It's so freakin' amazing.

So, then Dave starts over *again*, and he says the thing about don't look at each other. And again, they kind of look at each other, but now they do seem to know better. And *then* Dave adds,

```
                        DAVE

    God. You know, you guys sit there. You in your stupid
    designer tie, and you in your dumb-ass glasses and
    imported bottle of water!
```

Which is literally what they have. Bob's got on a tie, the other dude's got his glasses around his neck and he's drinking Perrier, or something. And they're like, what the fuck? But they still don't speak. So Dave keeps going . . .

```
    You're just sitting there looking down at the lowly
    actor on the stage, getting off on your power trip.
    But you know what? Fuck you. I don't need to be in
    your stupid, dumb-ass sitcom. It's fucking retarded.
    It's not funny. You know what? I read it. It's never
    going to work. Fuck you guys! Fuck you!
```

Then Dave storms out of the room, and he slams the door behind him. And the producers, like the rest of us, are just sitting there shell-shocked.

```
                        PRODUCERS

    Whoa, that was weird. What was that? Right?
```

And then all of a sudden, Dave pops his head back into the room and with glee he proudly proclaims,

<pre>
                        DAVE
      Aaand scene.
</pre>

And the producers start applauding and praising him. Then Dave calls out,

<pre>
                        DAVE
      NOOOO!
</pre>

I mean this dude was STILL in the monologue at the end when he walked back in. (And if you don't know, "and scene" is how some performers let people know their scene has come to an end.) So when Dave comes back in and says "Aaand scene" and even *that* was part of the monologue, it blew my mind. Who does that? Bob and Dave, that's who.

Then, of course, Dave dives right back in from the top . . .

<pre>
                        DAVE
      God, okay.
      Let me start again.
      Can I use this chair?
</pre>

And one of the producers stops him,

<pre>
      No kid, kid, we've seen enough. You got the goods!
</pre>

The Audition is the pinnacle of sketch for me. It is my jam. It is my straight jelly. It is my Fluffernutter. It is my turducken. It is my pie-caken. (Which, if you have not tried, is excellent, and is exactly what you think it is. It is a pie on top of a cake, on top of another cake.) I gotta tell you, it's at the top of my list. It's truly one of the best sketches ever. Like ever. Like all time.

This sketch contains *many* of the concepts and tools that we've shared along the way. It has the *who*, the *where*, the *what*, and the *other what*. It has heightening. It has yes-anding. On the weirdness scale of 1 to 100, the setup is maybe only a 6, but where it goes is 457. And when it ends, it is perfect Aristotle: It's unexpected and inevitable.

It encompasses everything I love about sketch comedy. This is like the *Mona Lisa* of simple setups, the *David* of turns, and the *Winged Victory* of payoffs . . . all rolled into one giant magical tree of every kind of fruit I love.

Okay, so that's a lot of similes, but it's just *that* deserving.

And with hard work and dedication, focus and passion, this level of sketch is one that sketch writers and performers I hope aspire to reach.

Now, I know I told you that this was a *Hey You Can't Do That* moment. But, you know what? This sketch is such a masterpiece, it's so grand, so perfectionals . . . I'm going to change things up a bit and say that this sketch, *this sketch,* should maybe instead be called a

hey you can . . .

and you should . . .

do that moment.

Thank you for joining us on this journey through the art and craft of humor.

Aaand scene.

INDEX